Universal Fascism

Universal Fascism

THE THEORY AND PRACTICE OF THE

FASCIST INTERNATIONAL, 1928–1936

Michael Arthur Ledeen

NEW YORK | HOWARD FERTIG 1972

Library of Congress Cataloging in Publication Data
Ledeen, Michael Arthur, 1941–
    Universal fascism.
    Bibliography: p.
    1. Fascism—Italy   2. Youth movement—Italy.
    3. Fascism.   I. Title.
DG571.L39   320.5'33'0945   70-185794

TO MY FAMILY

ACKNOWLEDGMENTS

Most of the research for this book was carried out in Italy between September, 1966, and September, 1967, as a result of a grant from the Foreign Area Fellowship Program of the American Council of Learned Societies and the Social Science Research Council, and I wish to acknowledge my gratitude to those bodies for their generous support. In addition to supporting my research activities, the Foreign Area Fellowship Program also enabled me to further my studies of the German and Italian languages before embarking on this project. Needless to say that linguistic training greatly facilitated the research for this study.

It is impossible adequately to express my gratitude and affection for the staffs of two great research facilities in Italy, the Biblioteca Nazionale Centrale of Florence, and the Archivio Centrale dello Stato in Rome. In particular, I wish to thank Signor R. Baglioni of the Florence Library, who patiently acquainted me with the bibliography of Italian fascism, and Dottore Costanzo Casucci of the Archive in Rome, who generously suggested lines of inquiry which had not occurred to me, and who made my many visits to the Archive both productive and enjoyable.

The Graduate School of Washington University, St. Louis, made it possible for me to return to Rome for the summer of 1968, to complete my research.

To Professor Stuart Woolf, Professor Giorgio Spini, Professor Renzo De Felice, and Professor Irving Louis Horowitz, I owe the benefit of hours of constructive criticism and suggestions.

Finally, I should like to thank Professor George L. Mosse for having suggested this fascinating topic in the first place, and for having patiently helped and encouraged me throughout the long period of research and writing.

CONTENTS

/\\/\\/\ The past five to ten years have seen a great resurgence of interest in the study of fascism. Scholars from a widely diverse range of countries and disciplines have been attracted to this fascinating and still largely unanalyzed phenomenon of our century. For many of these scholars, fascism is interesting because it seems to represent a dramatic and mysterious break with Western traditions and political behavior, and stands as a momentary plunge into darkness by an otherwise civilized and rational world. Such was the view of Benedetto Croce, who for years regarded his own country's adventure with fascism as a temporary interlude in Italian history, representing a momentary imposition of foreign ideas on his people.[1] For those who hold to such a position, fascism is considered an aberration of the "normal" flow of history, something to be studied as one studies abnormal psychology, as an example of the potential for deviance of the human animal.

Other students of fascism have come to view this phenomenon as a vastly successful movement which dominated European politics between the two wars to such an extent that the period warrants the label, "the fascist epoch." Scholars like Ernst Nolte, Stuart Woolf, and George L. Mosse[2] have attempted to show that fascism became the characteristic form of political behavior for a significant proportion of the European populace between the wars, and have argued further that such a widespread phenomenon cannot be understood unless it is viewed as part of a long tradition directed against earlier modes of thought and behavior. Consequently, these men have treated fascism as a part of the Western political tradition rather than as a radical break with the past.

This dispute is a serious one, and the adoption of one position at the expense of the other affects the kind of scholarship one pursues in attempting to understand fascism. If we accept the view that fascism was imposed upon various European peoples, or represents a break in the continuity of a people's history, then the focus of the analysis will perforce be directed towards an understanding of fascist leadership (in the early stages of the movement) and government. For this sort of investigation, the problem to be solved is how the fascist leaders were able to win support for their movement and regime, how they were able to discipline the population, and how they were able to maintain power. To a great extent the problem becomes one of biography, and many of the traditional analyses of fascism were directed primarily, if not exclusively, toward understanding the personalities and techniques of fascist leaders like Hitler and Goebbels in Germany, Mussolini and Ciano in Italy, and various quislings throughout Europe.

If, on the other hand, one views fascism as an integral part of the Western political tradition, then the question is much broader and more complicated, for one must attempt to explain why great numbers of people turned away from one set of political and ideological beliefs and adopted a different world-view. In this context, we are less interested in the oratorical skill of fascist leaders than in the emotional impact of fascist ideology and ideals. By stressing fascism's continuity with the past rather than its aberrant nature, one is compelled to deal with such elusive concepts as "national traditions," "popular culture," and finally the "climate of opinion" or, as Burckhardt called it, the "spirit of an age."

These are often dangerous tools for an historian to use, yet in the present case such an approach seems to be the only acceptable one. The shortcomings of the traditional methods, dealing primarily with the various pronouncements of fascist leaders and the biographical details of the lives of "great men," have long since been demonstrated. If fascism is to be properly understood, we must attempt, in our imperfect and groping way, to explain its popular appeal. Millions of Europeans enthusiastically embraced fascist doctrines in the period between the two world wars, and one would have to hold a dismal view of human nature to believe that so many men marched to their deaths solely because they had been hypnotized by the rhetoric of gifted orators and manipulated by skillful propagandists. It seems more plausible to attempt to explain their enthusiasm by treating them as believers in the rightness of a fascist cause which had a coherent ideological appeal to a great many people.

In what follows we shall examine one of the most important elements in the appeal of fascism, the notion that the world was about to undergo a complete transformation, and that this transformation would be brought about in the name of, and by the energies of, European fascist youth. In dealing with the history of this element of fascist rhetoric, we are making the assumption that fascist ideas were in fact taken seriously by many in the period between the two wars.

The content of fascist ideology will be discussed more thoroughly in what follows, but since this question has been hotly debated between scholars of the period, it is necessary to clarify my own position at the outset.

Denis Mack Smith, to take the case of one of the most distinguished historians of Italy, has suggested that "the only original contribution of fascism to politics was probably the technique of castor oil."[3] Mack Smith has deliberately exaggerated the lack of any major intellectual innovation within fascist rhetoric, yet his argument is a serious one. If one looks only at the speeches and writings of fascist leaders, one is hardpressed to find anything resembling the major political philosophies of the past: liberalism, socialism, or even the reactionary ideologies of the nineteenth and twentieth centuries. Yet fascism's followers believed that it represented a new outlook and a new spirit, and they attempted to piece together the often contradictory and incoherent observations of their leaders into a consistent world-view. Our primary concern in what follows will be with the ideas and enthusiasm of these devotees. Since the focus of this book is on the world-view of the followers of fascism, the claims of fascist leaders and the writings of fascist philosophers will often be relegated to a position of secondary importance.

This means that little space has been devoted to the theories of the leading philosophical figures in the history of Italian fascism, such as Giovanni Gentile and Ugo Spirito. Figures like Spirito and Gentile will enter our story only insofar as they served as centers for the crystallization of support for, or resistance to, the regime. In other words, we will be concerned more with the effect that their ideas had on fascist opinion than with the "pure form" of their ideas *per se*. Indeed, very few people had read the variations of Hegelian Idealism proffered by these two philosophers of fascism, and fewer still were capable of understanding them.

The focus of this study, then, is on a particular segment of Italian fascist society, and the effects of the ideas it advocated. We will be primarily concerned with educated young fascists, mostly intellectuals, in the late twenties and thirties. These young Italians and their ideas have received very sparse treatment from scholars, especially non-Italian intellectuals. Even in Italy, with the exception of two polemical volumes written by members of the generation which came of age under Mussolini,[4] the literature on the attitudes of fascist youth is virtually nonexistent. This lacuna is a serious one, for the first generation

raised by the Fascist Regime offers the historian a unique opportunity to test the viability of the regime itself. What better way
is there to gauge the popularity of the Fascist State than to see
if it was successful in indoctrinating its young people?

An investigation of this "fascist generation" reveals a striking
failure by Mussolini's Italy to win the unqualified allegiance of
young fascist intellectuals. This is all the more significant when
it is recalled that the court philosopher of fascism, Giovanni
Gentile, had himself organized the educational reforms in the
early twenties which were to have guaranteed the effective
"fascistization" of the Italian schools, and thus provided for the
assimilation of Italian youth into the fascist order.[5] Furthermore,
as we shall soon see, these young Italians were not only dis-
contented with the actual structure of the regime but considered
fascism's most signal failure to have been the inability to generate a meaningful doctrine, a philosophy of fascism which would
enable them to pursue the path of a genuine transformation of
the modern world. They therefore attempted to formulate such
an all-encompassing doctrine themselves, which they called the
doctrine of *fascismo universale*—the theory of universal fascism.

Before considering the framework within which this transformation of fascism was proposed, a few words must be said
about the significance of the rhetoric in which such a reconstitution of the world was couched. As we shall see, the adherents
of *fascismo universale* argued that fascism had failed to liberate
the creative energies of the Italian people. Their complaint was
that fascism had not provided a spiritual unity, a coherence of
vision, which could offer the Italian people a feeling of cohesion
and creative strength and so enable them once again to civilize
the world. This fascist mission was repeatedly linked with what
fascists took to be the civilizing heritage of Italy. Again and
again fascist intellectuals argued that Italy had provided the
West with Roman law, Roman Catholicism, and the intellectual

vision of the Renaissance, and that fascism must take its place in
that chain of heroic contributions to Western civilization.

These attacks on fascism's failure to provide a meaningful
world-view for Italians, and the parallel claim that it had failed
to liberate the creative energies of the Italian people, were not
new either to Italian history or to western European politics in
the modern period. Indeed, this kind of cultural criticism of
political organizations is one of the fundamental strands of the
intellectual history of the modern era. Fritz Stern has called the
phenomenon "the politics of cultural despair,"[6] and what is so
interesting about its appearance in Italy is that this sort of
criticism has traditionally been linked to the *origins* of the
fascist movements throughout Europe. Consequently, its existence as a critique within fascism in the second decade of its rule
warrants some consideration.

The ideology of cultural despair made its appearance in western Europe as an attack upon the failure of national unification
to achieve more than a merely institutionally coherent national
community. In Italian historiography this question has become
known as the problem of the continuity of the *Risorgimento*
and, as John Thayer has shown, the charge that Italy abandoned
the heroic ideals of the Garibaldian epoch once unification had
been achieved played a major role in driving Italy into an
interventionist position in the First World War.[7] Further, the
notion that post-*Risorgimento* politics were in some sense a
betrayal of the heroism of Garibaldi and the Thousand and of
the martyrs of the wars of the *Risorgimento* played a pivotal
role in mobilizing popular support for the First World War, for
D'Annunzio's exploits afterwards, and for Mussolini's young
fascist movement.[8] In a very significant sense, fascism was
supposed to have been a vindication of the *Risorgimento*. And
just as national unification had failed to satisfy the demands for
cultural elevation and creative liberation after the struggles of

the *Risorgimento*, so the establishment of fascist hegemony failed
to satisfy the very same demands for many young Italians.

Mussolini's problems were even deeper than those of the post-
Risorgimento politicians, for Giolitti and his allies had never
claimed to be the leaders of a revolution, let alone a revolution
of the Italian spirit. Indeed, the entire emphasis of the Giolittian
era had been on a normalization of Italian life and a definite
toning down of the tempo and intensity of politics. Mussolini,
however, had been swept into power by a group of disgruntled
enragés, many of whom insisted that the very spirit of Italy be
restored to its former greatness. Thus, while the leaders of the
post-*Risorgimento* could call for normalization, Mussolini was
forced to make constant obeisance toward those who, like the
futurists, demanded a creative explosion in Italy. The mood of
this heady enterprise has been captured very well by Nolte:

> . . . there was more to fascism than *only* castor oil and trun-
> cheons; it also meant, once victory had been achieved, the en-
> thusiasm of reconstruction, the zest of going to work, in which
> many of the best energies of the young people's urge to action
> found a home. That Italian life needed a profound renewal, that
> Italy must at last become a modern state, that there must be an
> end to bureaucratic dilatoriness, had been repeated much too
> often during the past thirty years for this new outlook not to
> have also inspired fascism.
> Bold words are sure to find an echo in young hearts—and was
> not Mussolini's promise, "In ten years, my comrades, Italy will
> be unrecognizable" truly a bold one?[9]

Mussolini's words were indeed bold, but all too many could
see that the Fascist Regime in the late twenties and early thirties
was far removed from that vision of heroic grandeur which
animated so many fascists. We shall have occasion to investigate
the results of their protest against a fascism which they felt
had grown old and stale in power, and which consequently

needed the rejuvenating force of youth to restore it to its state
of revolutionary health.

The protest against an aging and unsuccessful Fascist Regime
was not to be limited to a restoration of Italian fascism's revolutionary spirit. The young fascists who agitated on behalf of
fascismo universale were convinced that fascism represented the
destiny of the world, and that in the act of rejuvenating Mussolini's Italy they had to provide a doctrine for the rest of
Europe. This represented a demand for a real transformation of
the goals of the regime, for Mussolini had repeatedly voiced his
belief that fascism was a uniquely Italian phenomenon, tied to
Italy's experiences during and immediately after the Great War,
and therefore not "merchandise for export." The thirties saw a
renunciation of this slogan, and an adoption of many of the
goals originally put forward by the spokesmen for universal
fascism. Indeed, not only did the regime change its views on the
scope of fascism's relevance, but it finally embarked upon a
path of cooperation with foreign fascisms, and attempted to
organize a Fascist International in the middle thirties.

The doctrines of universal fascism therefore gained a place
within the policies of Italian fascism, and also exerted a certain
effect outside the boundaries of the Italian peninsula. It even
appeared for a while that a Fascist International might become
a significant force in Europe, for when an international congress
of fascist movements was held in Switzerland in the winter of
1934, representatives from all over the continent attended. Support for the organization of a Fascist International was widespread, and the story of this attempt tells us much about the
nature of fascism, both within and beyond the confines of Italy.
A consideration of fascism as an international movement helps
us to step outside the context within which it has been traditionally analyzed, and suggests, among other things, that fascist
leaders were sometimes unaware of the true popularity and
dimension of their movements.

Neither the doctrines of *fascismo universale* nor the attempt to organize a Fascist International have received any extended treatment by scholars of fascism. One possible reason is that much of the material on these questions has only recently become accessible in Italian archives, and that such material as was available to scholars was scattered throughout the country. They do, however, represent important components of both the Italian Fascist Regime and fascism as a European movement in the 1930's. Further, an investigation of these phenomena enables us to set fascism in better perspective as a European event, since the Montreux Congress, and the debates over the Fascist International throughout Europe, exposed several intense conflicts between various schools of fascism. These differences have often been obscured by attempts to present European fascism as a coherent movement, based on common beliefs, and as a common reaction to the European crisis of the period. Our investigation suggests rather that there were some very basic differences between various kinds of fascism, differences which will be discussed at some length.

The attempt to create an organization for the advancement of international fascism points to a significance which many historians have denied to Mussolini's venture in Italy. In the thirties, the Italian Duce often claimed that a new cycle was opening up in the history of Europe, and he believed that the new period would be characterized by a move toward fascist principles and institutions throughout the continent. The "fascistization" of the old continent did not take place, but before Hitler's Germany emerged as a dominant force in Europe one might well have foreseen such a development. The appearance of fascist movements in virtually every European country pointed to the attractiveness of the new ideology, and the majority of these movements pointed in turn to Mussolini's Italy as their major inspiration.

The ideology which inspired many European fascists was the

product of a revolt against fascist institutions and leaders in Italy, and much of the appeal of fascism as a model for other national movements stems from the heavy redrafting of fascist doctrine in the late twenties and early thirties. The youthful criticism of fascism, the subsequent elaboration of the doctrines of *fascismo universale*, and the attempt to organize a Fascist International together represent a significant episode not only within the boundaries of Italian history but in the broader context of European society.

All of this will no doubt seem bizarre to those who share the traditional conception of fascism as *opera buffa*, a phenomenon linked intimately with the basic theatricality of Italian politics and the personality of Mussolini, seen as the great chorus master of a political melodrama. Those who, like Mack Smith, consider fascism to have been nothing more than a facade for the ambitions of the leaders, render a more serious conception incomprehensible.[10] Yet it should be noted that one of the greatest Italian historians, Federico Chabod, believed that there could have been genuinely revolutionary elements within fascism, and that the possibility for a profound reconstitution of Italian society existed within Italian fascist doctrines:

> The two themes contained in both the laws and the speeches of Mussolini [in the early thirties], that is, "social justice" and "the expansion [of fascism] in the world," in fact lend themselves to two different interpretations. Must the new system be used as an instrument in the struggle for a nationalist politics, or can it really serve to provoke a radical transformation of the structure of Italian society, that is, to realize the social justice of which so much was spoken? . . . [Fascist Corporatism] ended by provoking and reawakening a new interest in fascism, especially among the young. Can fascism therefore contain within itself elements of growth which permit it to go beyond the purely dictatorial phase? . . . What is at its base? Is it only words, or something new. . . .?[11]

Chabod noted that all hopes for this social transformation ended when Mussolini embarked on foreign adventures in the late thirties. But he was not able to conclude that the potential for change which fascism seemed to contain was therefore a mirage. Rather, it does not seem unreasonable to argue that fascism contained various potentialities and that it might well have developed in another direction. Its final incarnation as a partner in the Axis with Hitler's Germany must not blind us to the significant voices within Italy calling for quite a different development.

In what follows, then, we shall examine the development of the movement for *fascismo universale* from the beginnings of the ideology to the attempt to organize a Fascist International, and beyond that abortive attempt to the dissolution of the movement in the late thirties.

Universal Fascism

CHAPTER ONE

Fascism and Youth

/\.V.V.\ In the middle of the nineteenth century Mazzini directed a call to a new generation of Italians to destroy the aged and corrupt Hapsburg Empire, and so produce a "Young Italy" which would act as both guide and symbol for a new order on the European continent. A decadent Europe would thus be revivified by Italian vitality and genius. In this ideological framework, "youth" was elevated to the status of a national principle. Distinctions were made between "young" and "old" nations to describe their relative vigor, creativity, and "vitality," a viewpoint which became an integral part of European fascism in general, and Italian fascism in particular. For these movements, fascism represented an expression of the "youth" of the nation, "youth" here meaning a spiritual principle, and not simply a group of young people.*

This elevation of Youth to an exalted position in the rhetoric of fascism has a long European tradition. Common to much of the romantic movement, the ideological lionization of Youth had been strongly reinforced in Italy by the poet-warrior Gabriele D'Annunzio, who had sung its praises throughout the Great War, and who himself came to symbolize the vitality and creativity of Youth for many Italians.[1] It is not insignificant that the first great surge of popular sentiment toward Mussolini's

* In what follows, "Youth" will stand for the principle, whereas "youth" (lower case) is used for the group of young people.

newly founded fascist movement occurred when he declared
himself in complete support of D'Annunzio's occupation of
Fiume, and the emphasis on "youthfulness" was to be a consistent theme throughout the convoluted path of fascist ideology. From the early support of D'Annunzio to the fall of
fascism in its final incarnation, the Republic of Salò, Benito
Mussolini declared himself to be the spokesman of Youth—a
young Italy, a young Europe, and a young fascism.

This concept of Youth was set against the decadence and
senility of the contemporary world, as well as against its arti-
ficiality and cynicism. Thus, in opposition to the "old Europe,"
the Europe of the Versailles Pact and the "mutilated" Italian
victory in the Great War, fascist Italy was hailed as the first
step in the inauguration of a new order—a new order to be
brought about by the revolution of the spiritually young.

In addition to its ties with the chiliastic visions of Mazzini
and the swashbuckling escapades of D'Annunzio, the *Weltanschauung* of Youth was strongly reinforced by the spokesmen
of futurism, with their attendant enthusiasm for modernity and
change.[2] An uneasy alliance existed throughout much of the
fascist period between fascists and futurists, and Marinetti himself often claimed to have been one of the originators of the
fascist movement—a claim which was echoed by many acute
observers of the period. The great Neapolitan radical syndicalist
Arturo Labriola, for example, would argue in 1923:

> When our youth is not D'Annunzian it is Marinettian . . . Mari-
> netti is the second intellectual father of this church. It is he who
> inculcated in the youth the cult of force, the scorn of human
> sentiments . . . the real basis for the conflict between *Popolari*
> [members of the Catholic Party] and fascists is the implicit ad-
> hesion of the latter to the "pagan" conception of Marinetti.[3]

Many considered futurism the "official" artistic and literary
movement of fascism, and while this is a considerable exaggera-

tion, it is certainly true that the futurists represented an important and extremely vocal segment of Italian cultural life under
fascism. Futurism provided a certain impetus for some of the
intensely patriotic and militaristic slogans of the regime. In
particular, its famous slogan, "We want to glorify war, the
only hygiene of the world"[4] was highly congenial to fascism.

The futurists spoke for the spirit of Youth, for an ardent,
exuberant, spontaneous, and creative force which they felt had
been suppressed in Italy for decades. All too often they have
been treated as eccentric epiphenomena of Italian culture; in
fact, many of their apparently *outré* ideas were to reverberate
with considerable force within the political milieu. One such was
the demand for the constitution of an organized youthful body
which could criticize the institutions and ideas of the older
generations, and thus provide the nation with an ever-abundant
supply of fresh ideas to guide the Italian people.

Implicit in this demand was a critique of the old way of
doing things, and Marinetti and the futurists more than once
voiced their disgust with parliamentary government, a system
which seemed to them to reward survival rather than youthful
vigor and creativity. In their eyes, parliamentary institutions
represented a repository for the old men of the society, a place
where the ideas of the past were voiced, and consequently
where thoughts directed toward revivification and dramatic
transformation could find little or no support. As Marinetti put
it in a speech delivered in Florence early in October, 1919:

> The Senate represents a constant homage to the wisdom of the
> elders in the story of the people . . . the concept of the Senate,
> similar to that of the chorus in Greek tragedy, has singularly
> weighed down, involved, retarded, and bureaucratized the spirit-
> ual and material progress of the race.[5]

This critique, which may be taken as paradigmatic of much
of the resentment against the older generations during the fascist

period, led to a demand for a method by which youthful originality and spontaneity could make itself felt within the government. For Marinetti, the importance of such an idea was that it
would not be modeled on other parliamentary organizations,
since that would simply enlarge the hated bureaucracy even
further. He therefore called for the creation of a new body,
which he proposed should be called *L'Eccitatorio* (literally,
"The Exciter"), composed of a small number of young men
(less than thirty years old) which would serve as a stimulus and
corrective to the tendencies of the bureaucracy. Its task would
be not so much to check and control the Parliament as to stimulate it along more creative lines.

> Behold the conception of the Exciter, an animating, simplifying,
> and accelerating organ, which . . . will be the best defense of
> youth and the best guarantee of progress and high spirituality.
> I dream in Italy of a Government of specialists excited by a
> Council of young people, instead of the actual Parliament of
> incompetent orators and infirm scholars. . . .[6]

Warning against the grave danger of permitting such a body to
grow old, Marinetti closed his oration by calling for a group of
students and futurist *Arditi* (former shock troops) to form
such an organization.

The notion of an organization alongside the government to
aid in the formulation of policy fitted in with the critique of the
elephantine nature of the modern bureaucratic State. And such
a critique was highly congenial to Mussolini, whose attacks on
the bureaucratic "State of Moloch" had been intense for some
time.[7] During the early years of the fascist movement, from
1919 up to the outbreak of the Matteotti crisis in 1924, there
was considerable interest among fascist leaders in the possibility
of establishing some kind of advisory council of the sort Marinetti had in mind. The so-called Competence Groups (*Gruppi
di competenza*), established by the fundamental organizing arti-

cles of the Fascist Party (the *Statuto-Regolamento generale del PNF*) of December, 1921, were strikingly similar to Marinetti's plea for a council of creative youth:

> Article 15. The Competence Groups have the goal of grouping fascist intelligence and capacities according to specialized attitudes and talents, in such a way as to render possible the study of whatever political, economic, or social problem may interest the nation, the region, the province, or the commune, and guaranteeing precisely with the security of competence a minimum of talent and practical success to the study itself. From the reciprocal recognition of the components of the Competence Groups will spring up automatically indications of how the infinite manifestations of fascist activity can best be utilized, so that *the final result of the Competence Groups will be to offer a most useful selection, both in the field of ideas and in that of the men who will have to apply those ideas on a practical level.* [my italics][8]

The scope of the groups was exceedingly large, including experts in railroads, urban and interurban trams; in the postal, telephone, and telegraph services; in gas, electricity, and potable water services; and in medicine and pharmacy; it also included workers and professionals. But as well as representing a kind of talent search, the Competence Groups represented an attempt to recruit talented people who might otherwise not have been willing to enlist in Party ranks. They thus represented an attempt, of the sort advocated by Marinetti, to create structures parallel to those of the bureaucracy in order to stimulate the creation of new programs and rational attempts to solve problems.

The leader of the Competence Groups was Massimo Rocca, a former anarcho-syndicalist. While Rocca was not infused with the cult of Youth which had animated the proposals of the futurists,[9] he viewed the groups as the means by which a new elite was to be formed. The Competence Groups, for Rocca, offered a means whereby people who preferred to function more

or less independently could still make a substantial contribution
to the nation. These would include many who might otherwise
be lost to the State:

> It can be added that to persons of character, indeed of proven
> national faith, but who have always lived outside the Parties,
> today's demand [1923] to enlist in the ranks of fascism without
> any higher reason seems like an antipathetic servilism toward the
> victor. Enlistment, however, by means of support of the Compe-
> tence Groups assumes a more dignified aspect, and almost a char-
> acter of public utility.[10]

The Competence Groups were established as a sort of techno-
cratic adjunct to the Fascist Party, offering the national leadership an opportunity to draw upon their expertise and providing
the groups' personnel in turn with the chance to participate in
the Fascist Revolution without immersing themselves in political
activities. As such, they hardly represented a radical thrust
within the fascist order. Yet Rocca's conception of the role of
the groups was far more grandiose than one would gather from
a reading of the statutes which created these bodies. Rocca
hoped that in the long run they would become the nuclei for
a new parliamentary body, which would represent the various
scientific and technological organizations of the nation, from
businesses to factories, universities to trade unions. He therefore
foresaw the transformation of the Competence Groups into
Technical Councils (*Consigli Technici*), and hoped that these
might provide the basis for a real transformation of the Italian
political system.

The movement which Rocca and the Competence Groups
initiated in the early twenties thus represented a serious challenge to those more traditional politicians who sought to con-
centrate the power of the country in the hands of the PNF
leadership. It is not surprising to find Party leaders opposing
Rocca from the beginning, and a spirited campaign led by Rocca
against squadrism in 1923 helped to deepen the gulf between

himself and the Party hierarchs. Rocca was expelled from the Party in 1923, briefly reinstated, then expelled again and ultimately driven from the country in 1924 as an enemy of the Fascist State.

Rocca's grandiose project perished when he left Italy. Although his successor as the head of the Competence Groups, Carlo Costamagna, urged Mussolini to establish the Technical Councils which Rocca had proposed, these never saw the light of day. Yet the idea of a new kind of political body, drawing upon the technological and scientific talent of Italy, later played a major role in the theory of the Corporate State. Rocca and the Competence Groups were the losers in one of the earliest intra-Party struggles of the Fascist Regime; but later events showed the durability of Rocca's conception.

Despite the early rejection of his program, ideas of the sort Rocca had proposed were to remain components of the intellectual debates among the fascist leaders for quite some time. For the immediate future, however, the abandoning of the project for the Competence Groups meant that notions of an independent and creative elite became increasingly centered on the more traditional institutions of Party and government. Where the futurists had called for the institutionalization of the genius of youth, the victors in the power struggles of the first decade of the regime attempted to integrate Italian youth into their own structures. Yet the rhetoric surrounding youth, and the concept of youth as a group more creative and more spontaneous than those of the bureaucratic leaders, was to remain. The legacy of Mazzini, D'Annunzio, and Marinetti remained a powerful one.

While a certain element in Italy had always paid lip service to these ideas, and while their popular appeal is evident, they remained somewhat outside the center of debates among fascist leaders until after the consolidation of the regime in the late twenties. With the resolution of the crisis following the Matteotti assassination, the problems of the perpetuation, rather than the establishment of fascism became paramount, and one of the most important of these problems was that of Italian youth. The government and Party moved with considerable speed to consolidate the various youth organizations under a single rubric, and concerns about education, discipline, and the assimilation of qualified young Italians ran at a high pitch.

The consolidation of fascist control over young Italians was not to be completed until the details of the Lateran Pact were worked out in 1929, but the most dramatic step in this direction before the agreement with the Church was taken in April, 1926, establishing the *Opera nazionale Balilla* (National Institute for the *Balilla*), the scope of which was the preparation of a new fascist generation. The description of its task leaves few questions about the intention of its creators. The *Balilla* was designed "to prepare the young . . . in such wise as to render them worthy of the new manner of Italian life."[11]

The *Balilla* and its allied structures, the *Fasci giovanile di combattimento* (Young Fascists) and the *Gruppi Universitari fascisti* (GUF) (University Fascist Groups), were designed to provide a constant flow of talent into the ranks of the Party. Indeed, from 1927 to 1932, the youth organizations provided the only source of new Party members, a fact which clearly indicates the importance of these structures to the regime. This comprehensive attempt to integrate successive generations into the framework of the Fascist State was quite reasonably viewed with alarm by the traditional guide and mentor of Italian youth, the Church. Limited by a law of January, 1927, to organizing activities for young people only in towns with populations exceeding 20,000, the Church found itself confronted by a fascist government which dissolved all Catholic youth organizations two months later.[12]

The details of the struggle between fascism and the Church

over the control of youth organizations need not concern us here, but it is important to note that the accords between Church and State of 1929 guaranteed the continuance of fascist organizations, and allowed for no Church competition in this sphere. Thus the regime was left an open field for the indoctrination of the young, and the thirties were to see a spectacular outbreak of activity supposed to guarantee that the first generation to come of age under fascism was adequately instilled with the ideals of the Duce. After the Lateran Pact, Mussolini told the Chamber of Deputies of the task which lay before them:

> . . . we need to give these youngsters the sense of virility, of power, of conquest; and above all we need to inspire them with our faith, and to inflame them with our hopes.[13]

It is hard to judge the effectiveness of fascist propaganda efforts on all levels of the Italian populace. So far as the university population was concerned, however, there is little doubt about the outcome of the attempt to create a new fascist intelligentsia: both from inside and outside fascist circles there is abundant testimony to the failure of the regime to integrate young fascist intellectuals into the new order.

This is not to say that many young Italian university students were overtly disloyal to the regime, for there is little evidence for such a claim. Yet it is clear that many indeed of those who represented the cream of the Italian university crop in the early 1930's were not rallying to the fascist banner with the enthusiasm that their leaders would have liked. And although they called themselves fascists, many university students showed a striking resistance to attempts at indoctrination. The gravity of the situation is well illustrated by a report to Mussolini from Carlo Scorza (head of the recently established *Fasci giovanile di combattimento* and secretary general of the *Gruppi Universitari fascisti*) on July 11, 1931, evaluating the situation after nearly a decade of fascist rule:

The masses in the universities are not yet what the Duce wants. . . .
Among university students those farthest from us are students of
Jurisprudence, Literature, Philosophy: the abstract subjects. Those
closest to us are, on the other hand, students of Medicine and
Engineering: the exact subjects.

I have found, among university students, a lively sense of autonomy in their relations with the Party, and a spirited disre-
gard of disciplinary and hierarchical bonds. . . .[14]

Scorza went on to complain about the ineffectiveness of
attempts by the Party to institute discipline, noting especially
that anti-fascist professors were frequently the most esteemed.
Consequently, the removal of "difficult" faculty members "does
not provide optimum results for fascist propaganda."[15] Worse
still, students tended to come under the influence of such teachers rather than of the GUF. Scorza pointed to the high per-
centage of anti-fascist assistants in the universities as evidence
for this claim.

As the solution to this dilemma, Scorza advocated a more
intensive indoctrination. His proposal was to create a new myth
for Italian youth, "because youth needs to believe passionately
in something, and to feel itself the center of something."[16] Having failed to integrate young Italians into the framework of the
Fascist State, the State must now find another ideology which
would win their allegiance.

This goal, however, was not fulfilled. In March, 1935, Achille
Starace, secretary of the Party, reported on the dismal confusion
which he found among the ranks of those dealing with fascist
education. Observing that this confusion had produced a negative attitude toward the regime on the part of youth, Starace
went on to elaborate this attitude itself in painful detail:

The school . . . appears to the young to be emptied of all educa-
tive content and of every ideal illumination and is therefore an

enemy, or at the very least is extraneous, to those forms of physi-
cal and spiritual educational activity towards which those
youngsters who grew up in the spiritual climate created by fascism feel themselves irresistibly drawn. . . .[17]

While the complaint is similar to Scorza's lament four years
earlier, Starace's remark is worth some consideration, since it is
all too easy to pass it over as typically flattering rhetoric
directed toward the Duce by an underling. In fact, there *was*
a remarkable amount of spontaneous activity going on among
young fascists during the early thirties, much of it, as we shall
soon see, urging Mussolini to drastically alter the course of fascist policy, and to permit a greater initiative and independence
to exist among the ranks of youth. The irony of the situation is
that many young fascists took the rhetoric of the Duce more
seriously than did the hierarchs of government and Party, and
thus attempts to discipline Italian youth were often frustrated
by youthful demands for a genuinely "fascist" university, culture, and State; demands which went beyond anything which
fascist leaders had in mind. In the chapters which follow we
shall see several examples of groups of young fascist intellectuals
who criticized the regime for its failure to live up to "genuine"
fascist principles. So, when Starace speaks of youthful antagonism to fascist schools, the most important element has been
omitted: the grounds on which that antagonism rested. Essentially, the critique was that fascism lacked coherence as an
ideology, and consequently that fascist culture was lacking in
the dynamism and vitality which was to have been its hallmark.
That was a far cry indeed from Starace, who demanded more
effective organization and regimentation from above, and the
elimination of disruptive elements from the schools.

The tone of frustration and desperation found in Starace's
letter permeated a large portion of the hierarchy's exchanges on
the subjects of youth and education, as well as a substantial

portion of the reflections of young Italians on their own situation.[18] As usual, Mussolini himself would provide the last word
on this complicated subject. Some weeks before his death, he
wryly observed that fascist rule had produced little lasting influence on the Italian people, a people which, in his memorable
phrase, "a tenacious therapy for twenty years has succeeded in
modifying only superficially."[19]

It is significant that such complaints were not restricted to
any particular period of fascist rule, but rather constituted a
basic theme of the *Ventennio*. Fascist hierarchs never achieved
the kind of control they wanted over young Italians, even
though they were virtually unchallenged after the signing of the
Concordat. This is all the more remarkable when one considers
the large number of rewards concentrated in the hands of the
national leaders. Not only could they reinforce the faith of
young fascists by giving them prizes for outstanding intellectual
and athletic performance, but they controlled the considerable
political patronage of the regime. Thus, those considered to be
of doubtful loyalty could be excluded from the better positions
when they left their educational training. This was especially
true of university students, yet the university was considered an
anti-fascist stronghold by some Party leaders.

We have already suggested one of the principal reasons for
the failure of fascist indoctrination: that the content of fascist
ideology was highly ambiguous. Given this haziness regarding
"acceptable" ideas, fascist leaders were frequently hardpressed
to determine who was an outright anti-fascist and who was
criticizing the regime in good faith. To some, "fascism" was
taken to be a dynamic movement rather than a set of fixed
principles, and many who were opposed to current practices
could criticize while still claiming to be good fascists. As a
result, a surprising quantity of critical writing and speech was
tolerated during the fascist period. Indeed, the panorama of

Italian cultural activities during the *Ventennio* is a variegated and often fascinating one.[20]

Fascist leaders were uncertain about precisely what constituted anti-fascist thinking, and they were even more dubious about what kind of action by young Italians should be punished. Even during the period of *Minculpop*—the repressive Ministry of Popular Culture—considerable freedom existed for young Italians who wanted to voice their opposition to the regime. This was especially true in those areas of the press which were either directed by, or concerned with, Italian youth. It was possible to say most things, provided that certain obeisances toward the person of Mussolini were made. Despite the claims of "totalitarianism" voiced by Mussolini and his comrades, the actual indoctrination of young Italians was not effective.

A further reason for the inefficacy of indoctrination was the duplication of structures designed to enlist youthful allegiances. The Party had its own youth organization, the *Fasci giovanile di combattimento*, while the *Opera nazionale Balilla* was under the control of the Ministry of Education. These were finally consolidated into the *Gioventù italiana del littorio*, under the personal supervision of the Party Secretary, in 1937. The double initiative meant, of course, that a consistent and coherent approach to the indoctrination of young people was rendered even more difficult.

The confusion which surrounded the leadership's approach to the entire question of youth is excellently demonstrated by the tentative attitude taken by the Party leaders toward the issue of punishment of young Party members who stepped out of line. In September, 1929, Secretary Turati issued a letter to the Provincial Federation Secretaries dealing with the question of disciplinary action. He stressed that the elimination of fascists from Party ranks (either by not renewing their membership or by taking away their membership cards) was an exceedingly

grave step, to be taken only in very serious cases. He went on
to deal with the case of youthful offenders:

> . . . one must proceed with unusual circumspection, remember-
> ing that youth, except in rare exceptions, is certainly a mitigating
> circumstance. . . .
> It is almost always a question of excellent elements which should
> not be lost, and toward which preventive action is better than
> punitive action.[21]

The message to the Provincial Secretaries was clear: they
were not to act against young fascists unless the violation was
very serious indeed. Whenever doubt existed, youth was to
receive the benefit of that doubt. There was, then, a very real
tolerance granted to young fascists, a kind of conditional freedom which assumed their good faith until drastic actions proved
otherwise.

This "freedom" granted Italian youth in the late 1920's and
early 1930's was, however, of a sort which imposed certain
requirements on their writing and speaking. Whatever was said
about the regime had to be cast in a fascist mold, and clearly
no explicitly anti-fascist writings were tolerated. Debates about
the nature of Italian society were acceptable so long as they
were clearly constructive, so long as they were aimed at an
improvement or "fulfillment" of fascism itself. The uniqueness
of those areas of the fascist press which were in the hands of
young people lay in the fact that, in general, the regime tended
not to question the good faith of the writers unless clear evi-
dences of anti-fascism were found.[22]

Throughout the fascist *Ventennio*, conflicts which before
Mussolini would have been described in the press in traditional
terms became "translated," so to speak, into a kind of fascist
"language." This is the essence of the methodology suggested
as early as 1926 by Antonio Gramsci:

. . . we must examine the stratifications of fascism itself because, given the totalitarian system which fascism tends to install, it will be within the breast of fascism itself that the conflicts will tend to arise, since they cannot appear in any other way.[23]

Given the nature of permissible public debate under Mussolini, there could be no problem which was not a "fascist" problem. Thus when we deal with the problem of Italian youth, it is perforce a fascist dilemma; and if Italian youth sought to transform its society, that transformation would perforce be a transformation of fascism itself.

The notion of Youth outlined earlier is one which had deep roots in the history of Italian political rhetoric, and its early identification with Mazzini's chiliastic vision of Italian unity is of considerable importance. The basic challenge to the second generation of fascists was, in a way, the same challenge which Mazzini and "Young Italy" had faced some seventy years earlier: the unification of Italy. Like Mazzini, many Italian fascists conceived of Italian unification in spiritual terms and looked for a national cohesion which would mean more than the imposition of a unified bureaucratic structure from Rome. At the same time, the desire of many hierarchs to impose the most highly unified structure possible set up an inner tension within the movement. The basic element of this tension is not unfamiliar to students of revolutionary movements: how does one liberate the creative energies of a revolution while at the same time guaranteeing the stability of the regime? In fascist Italy, this dilemma was heightened and dramatized by the concrete problem of indoctrinating and assimilating youth into the framework of the revolutionary State.

This problem of attracting young Italians to the side of the regime was one of the major preoccupations of Arnaldo Mussolini, brother of the Duce. Arnaldo Mussolini, two years younger than his brother, was a fascinating figure in his own right.

Immediately after the March on Rome, he became editor of
the PNF newspaper *Il Popolo d'Italia*. During the nine-year
period until his death in 1931, Arnaldo was one of his brother's
closest advisers, and showed himself particularly sensitive to the
problems of Italian youth. The slow, tortuous death of his eldest
son, Sandro Italico, from leukemia had a shattering impact upon
him and within a year and a half he followed the boy to his
grave. By the time of his own death Arnaldo had become
increasingly religious, and was immersed in the studies of mysticism that led to his founding of the School of Fascist Mysticism
in Milan dedicated to Sandro's memory. From his lofty journalistic pedestal as editor of the *Popolo d'Italia*, Arnaldo had been
looking to the young as a source of inspiration for the Fascist
Revolution. "There is," he had written in 1929, ". . . particularly among the young and the very young, a new conscious
force which will certainly make them better than us tomorrow."[24] And the following year he put this surprising notion in
even stronger terms: "Today Italian life lives and renews itself
for its youth . . . the young must feel themselves soldiers of the
spirit. . . ."[25]

For Arnaldo, the destiny of fascism lay in the hands of fascist
youth; but, even more important, that youth would be more
capable, more dynamic, and more creative than those who had
led the March on Rome. They could be all these things because
they had not been corrupted by nonfascist experience. Indeed,
they were viewed as far more than the next generation of
fascists: they were the moral force which alone could guarantee
the permanence and greatness of fascism itself.[26]

For Arnaldo, the task of youth was to elevate Italian life onto
a new moral plane. He believed that in the world of the future,
"political" problems as such would disappear, along with
"social" and "economic" ones. The new society, whose creation
awaited the creative force of fascist youth, would subsume all
such issues under the umbrella of fascist morality:

Fascism, rather than reduce the social problem to an algebraic question . . . has rendered it a moral problem; it has affirmed before all else the nobility of work, the obligation of production, the historical necessity of the Italian people, which must be and wants to be considered . . . as a pioneer of civilization and energy and not as an element of exploitation. . . .[27]

Since problems were now to be seen in moral terms, new criteria had to be firmly established, and the society had to recognize these moral criteria as paramount. The ideal of social justice must be both promulgated and institutionalized, and the new generation must dedicate itself to the fulfillment of this idea. For Arnaldo, fascism was taking part in a world war for justice; and "in this struggle for the justice of all, fascism can play its formidable role."[28]

The implication of all of this was that fascism's importance extended beyond the boundaries of the Italian peninsula. As Arnaldo put it, "If justice is to preside over the lives of men, it cannot fail to have a universal character."[29]

With this claim, Arnaldo Mussolini was formulating a position which ran counter to most of the official rhetoric of the first decade of fascism, and one which was to have important consequences in its second ten years of rule. The Duce had frequently stated his belief that fascism was a unique product of Italian genius, a phenomenon which had grown out of Italian problems and Italian culture. Arnaldo Mussolini was one of the first major fascist leaders to suggest that fascism might prove to be more than a purely national phenomenon, and his vision of a "universal" fascism was closely linked to his belief that the development of fascism would have to be achieved by fascist youth.

The fascist spirit—as the essence of a new civilization—is universal. It is based upon the trilogy: "Authority, order, and justice." An unstable, unquiet Europe, disintegrated in its civil millennarian function, restricted in the vague formulae of liberalism and democracy, cannot find its health, or better, its salvation, in any other way than a new order, which comprehends the necessity of single elements within the framework of the strong State, the sensibility of the crowd in the immutable truth of ideal politics. And it is for this reason that . . . [in all countries] we now see currents analogous to the fascist movement. . . .[30]

Arnaldo argued that such a universal spirit had not been provided by those who had marched on Rome in October, 1922. They had been products of a previous epoch, and as such had been inevitably tainted by old habits and the *arriviste* spirit of liberal politics. Those habits and that spirit had now to be destroyed and replaced by the new, universal fascist spirit. In the world of the future, this new spirit would transform society and illuminate all human relations.

Arnaldo's vision of a world transformed by a spirit of fascism transmitted by Italian youth was not restricted to merely rhetorical formulations. One of the most fascinating institutions of the fascist period, the School of Fascist Mysticism (*Scuola di Mistica Fascista*) founded in 1931 in Milan, was the creation of this prophet of the revolution of Youth, and it was a clear attempt to produce a youthful vanguard which would embody the spiritual qualities for which Arnaldo called with such urgency.

The School of Fascist Mysticism was, as we have seen, dedicated in memory of Arnaldo's son, Sandro Italico Mussolini. Sandro's death had a profound effect on his father, intensifying his Catholicism, and magnifying his faith in the messianic role of youth to the proportions of an obsession. The School of Fascist Mysticism was, in effect, to produce young Italians of the sort he believed his son would have been. In his own words, Sandro, "if he had been in this world, would certainly have spoken, in the name of youth and for youth, the new word of the Revolution."[31]

The School was then to have been a training ground for the

very best elements of Italian youth. Its orientation was elaborated by Arnaldo in his inaugural address on December 1, 1931.[32] He began by observing that youth was frequently eulogized, sometimes humiliated, but rarely profoundly understood. The new School of Fascist Mysticism was presumably unique in its understanding of the problems and potentialities of young Italians. Then he went on to explain what he meant by fascist "mysticism": "Mysticism," he said, "is a call to an ideal tradition which lives again, transformed and recreated in your program of young fascist renovators."

The importance of the entry of youth into society, Arnaldo reminded his audience, had a long and glorious history, dating back to the classical days of Athens, Sparta, and Rome. Fascist Italy had reinstituted the high honor of youth in the eyes of society, and consequently it was altogether natural that "fascist Italy, before every other necessity, feels the need to instill new life into the education of youth and . . . into national activities."[33]

Given Arnaldo's well-known belief that the generation raised under fascism would be far better equipped to carry out the goals of the Fascist Revolution than those currently in power, the aim of the School of Fascist Mysticism was very clear. It was designed to train those chosen to be the bearers of the revolutionary message to become the governors of tomorrow. The teachers and directors of the School thus had the high task of selecting only those genuinely committed to fascism at the most profound level:

The young man who lusts for the publication of all his writings and goes about collecting eulogies, puts his photograph on the frontispiece, loses himself in provincial ostentation; the young man who thinks he affirms his personality with gaudy calling cards . . . he who abandons himself in rhetoric . . . whoever, in short, lacks style will always be outside the spirit and the manners of fascism . . . they are not worthy of fascism. They are not worthy of you.[34]

Clearly the task of the School of Fascist Mysticism was a worthy one in the eyes of the regime. After the death of Arnaldo Mussolini in 1932, the name was changed to *La Scuola di Mistica Fascista Arnaldo Mussolini*, and remained invariably either in the hands of the Mussolini family itself (Vittorio Mussolini was the director for a brief period in the middle thirties), or with a reliable friend of the regime. In addition to training several hundred students each year, it performed all sorts of functions in the development of what might be termed "official" fascist culture, in the sense that its propaganda activities and public manifestations were always tied to official pronouncements. For example, the School held a series of demonstrations and lectures based on the theme "The Mysticism of War" ' 1935, aimed at instilling a warlike spirit in Italian youth. The journal *Dottrina Fascista* was a semi-official publication of the School, and its editor, Niccolò Gianni, was director of the School in 1937.[35]

The form taken by the School's activities by the late thirties would hardly have been comforting to its founder. Where Arnaldo had called for the development of a creative and dynamic spirit, the School itself had deteriorated into the most banal and arid sort of place. Its lack of creativity can best be illustrated by the very contented attitude toward it held by both the officials of *Minculpop* and the Party,[36] two institutions which by the late thirties had become as barren of any imagination and spontaneity as can be imagined. Instead of providing a constant stimulus and opportunities for development to young people, the School of Fascist Mysticism became integrated into an oppressive and bureaucratic framework where very little of intellectual worth emerged.

Despite the aridity of the institution he founded, the ideas of Arnaldo Mussolini were to be of major importance in the second decade of fascism. Both his concept of youth as a vanguard for fascist development and his notion that fascism had universal applicability were to have significant repercussions.

During the twenties, the Duce had frequently stated his belief that fascism was not "merchandise for export," but this slogan was soon discarded in the process of retooling the regime in the early thirties. By 1932 he could announce his confidence that

> . . . the twentieth century will be the century of fascism, it will be the century of Italian power, it will be the century in which Italy for the third time will return to being the guide for human civilization, because beyond our principles there is no salvation either for individuals or peoples. . . .[37]

Beneath the typical bravado of Mussolini's speech there were several serious problems. In the first place, the development of fascist doctrine in fascism's first decade had been centered around the notion that it was a uniquely Italian phenomenon. Now it was necessary to demonstrate the relevance of the Italian experience to the rest of the world. Secondly, and perhaps in the long run more significantly, fascism had failed to develop an ideology of sufficient coherence to make it "merchandise for export." This was the real thrust of Arnaldo's constant refrain that the radical development of fascism was to be left to the young, since it implied that the present leaders had not developed a philosophy of fascism. Indeed, in the first eight or ten years of his rule, Mussolini had often boasted that fascism was a system of action, free to improvise in order to solve the various problems it might confront.

In fascism's second decade the dictator felt the need to provide a set of principles, a political philosophy of fascism. And the development of fascist ideology necessarily entailed the integration of the new generation raised under fascism, the first generation in Europe to live in a fascist society.

Because the definition of fascist ideology was to transform

fascism's self-image from one of a national to an international phenomenon, and because this quest for ideological coherence took place during a period of major change in policy and personnel, the situation in the early 1930's was extremely fluid. Total control of the press was far from established, and the "fascistization" of the schools was an acknowledged failure. Further, the general "changing of the guard" which marked the period enabled many to speak out on subjects which might have been too delicate during the tenure of the previous bureaucracy. Finally, implicit in the search for doctrinal coherence was the admission that the fascist leaders had failed to arrive at durable solutions to Italy's (and now Europe's) problems. Thus even criticism of the previously untouchable "fascists of the first hour" could be ventured.

The ultimate formulation of official doctrine (in the famous Gentilean *Political Doctrine of Fascism* of 1935) is not of immediate importance to us here. What is significant is the widespread awareness of both Mussolini and educated Italians that fascism had failed in the signal task of providing a doctrine of wide applicability. Now Italy had to provide the model for the restructuring of the Western world. Fascism would therefore have to be an all-embracing system. Art and athletics, politics and architecture, commerce and literature would be equally relevant, for fascism would have to demonstrate its worth in every area of human endeavor.

The stage was therefore set for a major re-evaluation of fascist ideas and institutions. Fundamental to an understanding of the development of the ideologies which follow is the realization that many Italians looked to the thirties as a period which would see a dramatic transformation both of fascist doctrine and of the shape of the world. As we shall soon see, many embraced Arnaldo Mussolini's concept of a fascism which would have universal validity, and consequently the destiny of the entire Western world became a central fascist issue. The thirties would see a major expansion of intellectual activity within fascist ranks, as fascist theorists of all kinds attempted to show the ways in which the development of Italian fascism was relevant to the crisis then shaking the West to its foundations. Finally, Italian youth felt that it had a unique role to play in this twentieth-century drama, and spokesmen for Youth were not lacking as fascism moved into its second decade.

CHAPTER TWO

Youth and Universal Fascism

/v.v.\ Having survived nearly a decade which had seen Mussolini cope successfully with a variety of threats to his power, and with the resolution of the knotty problem of the relations between the Palazzo Venezia and the Vatican, the Fascist Regime entered the thirties with high hopes for the future. Apparently having weathered the domestic storms, the fascists were anxious to proceed with the consolidation of the dictatorship and the extension of fascist institutions throughout the various spheres of Italian society.

In this period, however, many voices were heard suggesting that those who had been pivotal in the leadership of the March on Rome and the establishment of the regime were unsuited for the new tasks. The future of fascism demanded new people and a new spirit, and that new spirit was invariably identified as the spirit of Youth.

Such proposals for change in the personnel and philosophy of fascism were made by some of the most influential and authoritative spokesmen for the Fascist Revolution, and would be echoed by many young Italians who were themselves anxious to guide the revolutionary ship on its future course. One principal focus for this agitation was to be found in the person of Giuseppe Bottai, born on September 3, 1895. One of the earliest fascists, Bottai earned a degree in jurisprudence and helped to found the Roman *Fascio*; he was elected a deputy in 1921 at the age of twenty-five, and served in the 26th, 27th, 28th, and 30th Legislatures. In 1926 he became undersecretary to the Minister of Corporations. He drafted the Labor Charter in 1927. In 1929 he became Minister of Corporations; in 1933 and 1934 he was president of the National Institute of Social Security, and for the following two years governor of Rome. At the end of 1936 he became Minister of National Education, and drafted a significant school reform bill known as the School Charter. He was active in promoting the extraordinary meeting of the Grand Council of Fascism on July 24–25, 1943, which overthrew Mussolini, and for which Bottai was condemned to death by the Special Court of Verona. He was later also sentenced to death by the High Court of Justice of Rome in 1945, but neither of these sentences was carried out, since Bottai had fled Italy upon the fall of fascism to join the French Foreign Legion at Sidi-Bel-Abbès under the name of Andrea Battaglia. When he was amnestied in December, 1947, Bottai returned to Italy to resume a journalistic career which he pursued with vigor until his death on January 19, 1959.[1]

Bottai held a significant place in the Fascist Regime, and his importance extended beyond the boundaries of the government. Through the pages of *Critica Fascista* (*Fascist Criticism*) in 1923 to 1945, Bottai was in the forefront of the effort to infuse Italian culture with a new vitality. In this sphere he was able to act with considerable energy and autonomy, and sought to encourage new lines of development, independent of the strict control which Party hierarchs were attempting to impose from above. After the consolidation of the dictatorship this was perhaps the only kind of activity in which such an initiative could take place. Bottai thus became the leader of a certain element within the ranks of fascism which tried to reform the cultural and educational structures. He himself spoke of his role in terms of the generation which fought in the Great War:

There is a generation which encountered Mussolini between 1915 and 1919, between trench and piazza, which has always subordinated its own will to his, but not destroyed it . . . which has always known how to renounce some of its own particular ideas, but not its own thinking. . . .[2]

This generation, Bottai's own, was the generation which had marched on Rome. It was loyal in the extreme, but jealously guarded its right to criticize the policies and postures of the Fascist State. For Bottai, this right to dissent from within was a "conditional autonomy,"[3] and he exercised this autonomy for the better part of his career.

It is thus of the utmost significance that we find the voice of Giuseppe Bottai among the rising chorus supporting the demand that the hierarchs step aside and let the new generation have its way. Bottai tied the rise of a new generation to a European-wide situation, a situation which now saw the young demanding a voice in the government of every European country. He gave his readers a sample of the dilemma in France by quoting from *Le Temps* on June 15, 1930:

Alas! It must be said that two generations have never been more completely separated than these two, between which the war opened a chasm . . . the ideal youth of 1930 . . . is, it appears, a realist, a creator, active, resolute, decided to triumph quickly . . . but also the ally of work. . . . He does not count only on violence. He prefers intelligence, audacity. . . .[4]

Bottai observed that the same characteristics were to be found in young Italians, but there was one major difference: Italy had established a young regime, whereas the French had not. In Italy, virtually all the members of the prewar generation had vanished from the national scene, whereas in France they were still at the helm. "The generations of fascism begin with Mussolini, the French youth are still under the attraction of Clemenceau."[5] This had major consequences in the types of crises generated in the two countries:

We are thus confronted with a problem of the younger [generation], which is a problem of preparation, of development, of maturity, while in France the restlessness of the youth will tomorrow be a problem of conquest.[6]

France had a "youth" problem, while Italy had to deal with a "younger" generation. This notion of the "young" and the "younger" had been formulated a few months earlier by Bottai in the pages of *Critica Fascista*[7] and was picked up by Mussolini himself in a statement dated January 21, 1930, entitled *"Punti fermi sui giovani"* (Firm bases on youth). In that statement, which reverberated throughout the press, Mussolini declared that "the regime is, and intends to remain, a regime of youth."[8] The dictator went on to give various illustrations of what he had in mind. In the first place, he wanted to keep the average age of its members as low as possible; for example, he said, given the choice between someone thirty years old and someone forty, all other things being equal he would prefer the thirty-year-old. Furthermore, the regime had to dedicate itself to the spiritual preparation of youth and Mussolini felt that this work was already well under way in the various fascist institutions dealing with young people.

It was this second element which most interested Bottai and his allies, and on February 1, 1930, Bottai spelled out his concern in the form of an exegesis of the Duce's text of eleven days before.

The Duce's statement had committed fascism to enlisting the support of Italian youth in its efforts, and saw in that youth the only means of guaranteeing the continuity of the Fascist Revolution. Bottai insisted, however, that one had to distinguish between "true" and "false" youth, between those who genuinely embodied the strong will and creativity which characterized the principle of Youth, and those who used their young age as an excuse for irresponsible behavior. For Bottai, "true" youth provided the only possible security for the future of fascism.

A regime which does not want to rigidify itself in a method, imprison itself in preconceptions, preclude every possibility of perfection and renovation of its own ruling class, must keep itself spiritually and practically in contact with the younger generation.[9]

Bottai claimed to have seen dramatic evidence of this necessity in the fall of the De Rivera regime in Spain, a collapse due, he said, to the great alienation of university youth from the regime. It seemed to Bottai that the Fascist State must open every possible avenue of access to "those who could not participate in the War and the Revolution."[10]

The generation which had fought in the Great War and created the Fascist State had performed a prodigious work; yet a new kind of labor lay ahead. A new spirit seemed to be awakening in Italy, which would transform the Italian people from "an instrument of history" into "the agent of a new history."[11]

The organization and education of the young, then, was of signal importance in the development of fascism as a State system. To this end, it was necessary to do more than introduce fascist techniques and fascist ideas into the school system: one must create "the fascist school." In so doing, however, one must avoid the danger of creating simply a new kind of confessional education. In the words of a contributor to Critica Fascista, "we must avoid catechizing youth."[12] The aim of the fascist school must be to develop the potentialities for creativity and responsible activity to the full, without forcing the students into a mold created by the older generation. The problem, as we know, is hardly unique to fascism, and struck home with special force in a nation which claimed to be the vanguard of Youth throughout Europe. It became accentuated even further when young Italians began to make the very same claims on their own behalf, and to criticize members of the regime for thinking in "outmoded" terms.

Bottai and his followers urgently searched for some way to guarantee lines of entry into the regime for those they considered the better members of the younger generation. While Mussolini's statement appeared to guarantee such people open access, the institutions established by the Party seemed to some to be heading toward the creation of a new sort of aristocracy, whose ranks would be closed to those who had not obtained a Party card at an early age. To protect against the Party leaders' tendency to seal off access to positions of power to those who had not seen the light of fascist wisdom at an early age, Bottai wrote a stinging article in the middle of October, 1930, entitled "*I Giovani nel partito*" (Youth in the Party).[13] This attempted to recall the spiritual necessities of the Revolution, and stressed that what was needed for fascism was "the minimum of formalism . . . and the maximum of spiritual intensity, voluntarism, of that spirit of sacrifice and heroism which is the fundamental and distinctive quality of the fascist character."

Any preconceived method of sorting out young fascists was therefore doomed from the start. Instead, the Party had to maintain the highest possible flexibility in establishing criteria of selection. Bottai attempted to put the issue in historical perspective by recalling that the various structures to educate and train youth had themselves resulted from a debate over the nature and role of the Party. The *Balilla*, GUF, and so forth had been proposed to guarantee that the Party not become closed to innovative elements. But the problem of the Party itself had merely been posed again in a new form, this time at a younger age level.

Bottai went even further in his criticism. The Party, he said, must represent the future, and as such must open itself up to a constant transfusion of new elements. Mussolini had proclaimed that fascism had entered upon a "new cycle," and for Bottai that new cycle must entail an affirmation of Youth. That affirmation had to be "not only an affirmation of men and jobs, but of spirit, of environment, of mentality."[14]

Involved here are many issues of paramount importance, given Bottai's role within the regime of trying to impart a certain independence and originality to the cultural and educational spheres. The claim he made struck at the very heart of the strength of the Party, for he was arguing in essence that much remained to be done within the Fascist State, and that the generation in power was not the group which would realize that task. This claim, found (as we have seen) in the speeches and articles of Arnaldo Mussolini, was made explicit in the pages of *Critica Fascista*, not only by Bottai but by other writers as well. One of the clearest formulations of this position is to be found in an article by Agostino Nasti (a member of the editorial staff of *Critica Fascista* and a close friend of Bottai) suggestively entitled *"Giovani, meno giovani, giovanissimi"* (Young, Younger, Youngest),[15] which appeared in December, 1930. After rehearsing the history of the Fascist Revolution, and calling attention to the fact that it was carried out by the young, Nasti turned his attention to the present situation. Italy in 1930, he said, found itself between two phases of the Revolution. The first phase, that of the preparation for fascism, had lasted throughout the war. The second, which realized the Revolution, had begun in 1919 and lasted until the present. Italian youth faced a major task in the future. "These young boys come in time to collect an inheritance which is neither light nor easy"— the task of expanding the Revolution beyond its present boundaries, the task of making fascism more than a local phenomenon.

> The work of the Revolution expands, and extends itself in ever greater circles of vibration . . . *the fascist State is not actualized, it is actualizing itself,* and for this actualization, which needs and absorbs the energies of our revolutionary youth, the generations immediately following will certainly be necessary. . . . [my italics].[16]

The thrust of Nasti's argument is clear: the generation in power at the moment has achieved one great task, but that which lies ahead is even greater, and will require the energies and mentality of a new generation for its achievement. The expansion of the scope of fascist activity entails both an opening up of fascist ranks, and the direction of a new wave of fascist leaders.

The basic theme of *Critica Fascista* was to endure until the destruction of the regime, and formed an essential part of the general demands of the new generation. Aside from the clear importance of this theme in the structure of the Fascist State, there is a further significance to the insistence that a new task lay ahead which could only be achieved by a new generation: it implies that this was a task as yet unformulated by the present hierarchs. What was that task? None other than the great mission often hinted at by Arnaldo Mussolini and others, and finally made explicit in the early 1930's by the Duce himself: the entry of fascism on a worldwide scale as a universal phenomenon.

Critica Fascista was not the only journal to see the connection between the role of fascist youth and the movement for universal fascism. Indeed, as we shall shortly see, it was far from being the first to recognize this relationship. But given the importance of Bottai, the link between the aspirations of fascist youth and the expansion of fascism to a universal level takes on added significance when it appears in the pages of *Critica Fascista*. Further, Bottai's position as a leader of the "loyal opposition" helps us to understand the role which the doctrine of universal fascism played within the political framework of fascist Italy.

By January, 1933, we find the theme of universal fascism emerging in quite some detail in the pages of Bottai's journal. Responding to a call for a sort of referendum on the future of fascism, Bottai stated his belief in the permanent nature of the Fascist Revolution, and his expectation that fascism's applicability would continue to expand beyond purely Italian boundaries. "Fascism," he wrote, "is the Revolution of the twentieth century."[17]

The transformation of fascism from a national to an international phenomenon was not simply a matter of ideological extension. Rather, Bottai argued, it derived from the realities of the twentieth-century world. Every state in the world was undergoing a crisis, and they were all turning towards fascism in an attempt to find a common solution to what had become a common problem. However, one must not jump from this to the conclusion that fascism of the specific form found in Italy was going to make itself manifest throughout the world. Rather, one must view fascism as an operative agent in the resolution of the worldwide crisis:

> Fascist thought has, by now, a universal circulation; it has entered into contact with a complex of doctrines, tendencies, aspirations, and habits, over which it has placed itself as a corrector and regulator, but from which it can do no less than collect an infinity of new vibrations. . . .[18]

It follows from this analysis that fascism itself will most likely undergo a substantial modification, derived from its contact with the world crisis. This conclusion strongly reinforced Bottai's previously announced conviction that the future lay with the young, and that the older generations were unable to shape fascism in the years that lay ahead.

In essence, then, Bottai's position was that fascism was to be viewed as a Revolution *in progress*, and that the infusion of the creative energies of a new generation was essential for this progress. Bottai would then naturally support any attempt on the part of young Italians to exert their influence upon the leaders, and would encourage the development of a certain independence of mind among the younger generation.

What set Bottai apart from many of his contemporaries was

not so much his emphasis on the value of a creative and energetic youth as his contention that the development of this youth was not a matter of Party indoctrination and training but rather of education and intellectual stimulation. The nature of the debate on this issue becomes clear if we consider its development in the pages of *Critica Fascista* during the period 1930–33. We shall consider the two poles of Bottai's lengthy polemic on this subject, first treating his initial formulation in 1930, then his defense in 1933.

The opening blast in Bottai's campaign on behalf of youth took place in the first issue of *Critica Fascista*, in the year 1930. In an article entitled *"Giovani e più giovani"* (Young and Younger), he noted that there was a "youth problem" all over the world, calling attention to unrest among the young in France, the Soviet Union, the United States, and even Switzerland.[19] He claimed that the only country in the world which had resolved this crisis in a straightforward manner was fascist Italy, where a young generation had seized power from an old one in 1922. In Italy, he argued, youth was indeed in power, since the fascist ruling class was young. In other countries, by contrast, there was a genuine clash of generations, a real war of young against old.

The question in Italy, therefore, was one of "the younger," *i più giovani*. This refers to the generation which had come of age during the first eight years of fascist rule. Bottai then quoted a journal (*L'Universale* of Florence) which had demanded the mandatory retirement of all men over the age of thirty, and observed that this was characteristic of a certain not uncommon state of mind:

> The State . . . is that described earlier: thirty is the median and living age of a great work of political, social, and economic reform. How . . . are the new generations to be incorporated? The mechanism exists and is known: *Balilla*, *Avanguardia*, Militia, and

Party. The mechanism is worth whatever it is worth, like any other. . . .[20]

Bottai felt it crucial that this mechanism not become the sole activity of the State in providing for the integration of youth into the ranks of the Revolution. After a lengthy and often heated debate during the course of the next three years, he spelled out his position with greater clarity in 1933. In March he proclaimed that "the problem of youth is the central problem of fascism."[21] Indeed, he viewed this problem as so urgent that, if it were not solved, "one might as well do nothing." And he went on to give a definition of "youth" which brought him into Arnaldo Mussolini's camp:

> Youth is a special condition of the spirit and of the conscience, which Fascism, Fascism-as-movement, Fascism-as-Revolution, must know how to value in its development . . . in order not to turn into a museum of conventional ideas. . . .[22]

Youth as a state of mind was essential to the development of a dynamic fascism. The problem was clear: one must utilize the progressive and dynamic force of youth in order to keep the Revolution alive. But what about the much-vaunted "mechanism" for assimilation? For Bottai, the organizations had all too often degenerated into a gigantic job-placement office where young position-seekers came to make their fortunes. Crying "Positions, positions, always positions," Bottai deplored this tendency toward easy bureaucratization of the youth organizations, and urged his compatriots to return to revolutionary principles. "Better an eccentric new idea," he maintained, "than an acceptable old one."[23]

Youth, then, was not being sufficiently encouraged or adequately trained to undertake the great tasks that lay ahead. On April 15 Bottai returned to the problem in answering his critics, and in so doing again called attention to the moral and spiritual elements of the crisis. The problem of the generations, he reiterated, was not simply a question of substituting young people for old; it was a question of introducing a new spirit and fresh ideas in places where old, stale concepts were prevalent.

> It is not true that a change of generation always in itself constitutes a step forward, if the new [generations] are not methodically prepared; if they are not given the feeling that the system, in which they are called to serve and act, is susceptible to development.[24]

A revolutionary generation had often been followed by a conservative one in the past, and it was of the utmost urgency to assure that this fate did not befall the Fascist Revolution. The question was one of developing a fascist tradition of education and culture that would provide for the integration of a sensitive and alert youth into the State. Bottai's description of the problem was typical of one who was preoccupied with questions of education:

> Between educating to the passive acceptance of the completed fact, and educating to the working acceptance of an indefinitely perfectionable order, there is a vast difference: that between stasis and movement.[25]

So, Italian youth was being actively encouraged to strike out in new directions by figures like Giuseppe Bottai and Arnaldo Mussolini. Further, as the bearer of the inheritance of the Fascist Revolution, these young people were conceived to be the generation which would carry the revolutionary tradition onto a universal plane. Young Italians were not to remain unmoved by such appeals as these. Among those to strike out upon a new path was none other than the son of the dictator, Vittorio Mussolini.

Vittorio was one of a sizable group of teen-age poets and writers who published an annual journal. The group, called

"Novismo," was primarily interested in the development of a truly fascist "culture," and their writings, which extended roughly from 1929 to 1935, reflected a strong anti-conformity, directed variously against the "old" mentality of fascist hierarchs, against futurism, even against the Church and such luminaries as the vice-secretary of the Party, Arturo Marpicati.[26] By the early thirties the group could claim several hundred adherents, with an organization extending throughout the country, and a feebly elaborated doctrine of "Novismo." The sense, if not the ideas, of this group can be judged from the following statement of September, 1933:

> Novismo is a movement of ideas which extends to all areas of human activity, which refutes dogmas, schemes, prejudices of all sorts. The only rule for its development: honest proposals....
> Novismo is national, but not chauvinistic: it puts man before citizen; humanity before Italy.
> Novismo acts for the intellectual and moral freedom of all. . . .[27]

"Novismo," in short, tried to embody some of the directions for which both Bottai and Arnaldo had called. It was an attempt, if unsophisticated, to establish a meaningful fascist culture which would extend beyond merely national boundaries to embrace Western civilization as a whole.

The historian Enzo Santarelli has recently observed that the "Novismo" group is a very difficult one to evaluate.[28] On the one hand, the presence of Vittorio Mussolini in their midst could have given them a feeling of independence which would explain much of their anti-conformist writings. On the other, his presence also raises some doubt as to the integrity of their motives. The group could well have been either a "trial balloon" by the regime to see how other young intellectuals would react, or a trap baited with Vittorio to lure anti-fascist intellectuals into the open. Whatever the explanation, the group was far from being the most outspoken in existence, and other, more independent groups remained virtually untouched by fascist censors.

Nevertheless, "Novismo" serves as a paradigm for numerous groups during the *Ventennio*. Many young intellectuals were seriously engaged in the exciting work of preparing for the century of fascism as they had been encouraged to do by their leaders. They were attempting to build an ideological model which would extend fascism's applicability to the boundaries of the world, and in so doing make Italy once again the guide for Western man in his search for an end to the crises which were besetting him. One of the most important of these young intellectuals was Gastone Silvano Spinetti, a young journalist who in 1936 edited the first general volume of the speeches and writings of his ideological *maestro*, Arnaldo Mussolini. Later in the decade, Spinetti joined the staff of *Popolo d' Italia* and did some work for the Ministry of Popular Culture (*Minculpop*). Throughout his career, Spinetti has remained an eloquent spokesman for his generation, and has continued to the present to defend the honesty with which many of his generation tried to "reform" fascism in the thirties. He describes his friends as "young people who, even if Italy had won the war, would have initiated and carried through a real revolution within fascism."[29] The nature of that "revolution" would have been the transformation of the regime into a universal movement, inspired by the values of Youth.

Spinetti's journalistic activities came to the fore around the latter part of 1932, about the same time that Vittorio Mussolini and the "Novismo" group were calling for the free play of fascist ideas. In January, 1933, Spinetti and his friend Giorgio Prosperi brought out a new journal called *La Sapienza*, directed by young intellectuals dedicated to the overthrow of Gentilean Idealism, and to the promulgation of an ideology of "universal fascism." *La Sapienza* called for the renovation of Italian fas-

cism and, in the spirit of countless other groups grown dissatisfied within a "revolutionary" regime, urged its countrymen to
return to the original source of revolutionary inspiration, the
"principles of 1919."[30] This return was viewed as a necessary
first step in recapturing the initial dynamism of fascism, a
dynamism which seemed distinctly lacking in the ranks of a
generation grown old and flabby in power. If fascism returned
to this original source of inspiration it would not only resolve
the Italian crisis, but indeed "within a century the world will be
fascist . . . given that universality is one of the characteristics of
European civilization which is essentially Roman."[31]

The return to the original fount was no easy matter. The
landscape, once barren of ideological flora, had become a tangle
of doctrinal growths of the most varying sorts, and without a
substantial pruning it seemed most difficult to find the original
seed. Rather than wind their way through this tangle of ideology, Spinetti and his *confrères* decided to cut through to the
root of the matter, and to attempt to eliminate the one ideological weed which they saw spreading on every side: the Idealist
doctrines of Giovanni Gentile. On May 14 and 15, 1933, the
staff of *La Sapienza*, aided by many of the futurists, organized
an "Anti-Idealist" Convention in Rome to demonstrate the
widespread opposition to Gentilean doctrines throughout Italy.
Declarations of support came from the length and breadth of
the peninsula, and included such leading intellectual figures as
Carlo Curcio, Guido Manacorda, Gino Arias, Emilio Bodrero,
and Ruggero Zangrandi.[32] These were all major figures in
fascist journalism, and some, like Curcio and Manacorda, held
university positions as well.

The main thrust of the young intellectuals' attack against the
philosopher of Castelvetrano was summarized in an article by
Prosperi the same month in *La Sapienza*. Idealism, Prosperi
argued, had failed to provide a coherent framework for the

development of fascism. It had attempted to defen
liberty but had in fact destroyed it. In attempting t
philosophical basis for fascism, Idealism instead had become
"integral Bolshevism."

> It was betrayed by its own logic: while wanting to identify mat-
> ter and spirit it murdered the spirit; while wanting to identify
> externality and internality it murdered internality; while wanting
> to identify nature and art it rendered art useless; while wanting
> to identify man and God it murdered God.[33]

The integrity of the individual had to be maintained but, for
the young editors of *La Sapienza*, individualism had also to be
overcome. To this end, the Anti-Idealist Convention was organized not simply to voice opposition to the doctrines of modern
Idealism but also to elaborate the possibilities for a new order.
Subjects under consideration at the Convention thus included
"Fascism as a Universal Movement," "Idealism and Bolshevism,"
and "The Necessity for a Cultural Revolution." Aside from the
polemics against Gentile, the central issue was the future course
of fascism. Prosperi put the issue clearly to his readers: "Too
many people still believe that fascism is just a revolution of the
government; too many people delude themselves in thinking
that the methods can leave the substance intact. . . ."[34] Instead
of merely transforming the structure of the governmental
apparatus, fascism was about to enter a new phase, which would
leave behind not only the methods of nonfascist government but
also the mentality of the old order:

> More than the expression of our times, we are in fact the pre-
> cursors of a new era, of a civilization which we will not hesitate
> to call fascist, because our value must not consist in being the
> first to have predicted the universal reaction, but in having nour-
> ished it and guided it, in having shaped our doctrine to it. . . .[35]

This new era, the era of fascism, would be characterized by
the spirit of Youth, a spirit clearly revolutionary in all areas

where the "old" mentality still held sway. The old mentality was symbolized by Gentile's variation of Idealism, the so-called "philosophy of the pure act," which for Spinetti and his friends was simply a flimsy copy of the Kantian and Hegelian traditions. Indeed, Gentile's philosophy had resulted in a kind of superscepticism, a complete denial of any objective criterion by which one could assess the *value* of anything. Worse still, by driving God out of the world, Gentile had eliminated the possibility of the perfectibility of either human society or the human spirit.

The new generation of fascists stood in opposition to this pessimistic monism. In December, 1934, Spinetti published a limited edition of a volume entitled *Fascismo Universale*. Written, as he put it, "by a youth for youth," this was to be the first in a series of works to appear each year in honor of the March on Rome. Reiterating his opposition to the destructive influence of Gentile, Spinetti repeated his belief that his own generation stood between two great epochs of human civilization. The entire world was undergoing a crisis, affecting all areas of life. Moreover this crisis, while manifesting itself in all spheres of human activity, was essentially a moral crisis, and could be resolved only by creating "new order in the world of the spirit."[36] This new order could only come from fascism.

> Fascism signifies not only a renewal of institutions, but also of culture and of souls; it signifies a norm of life: this is the sole reason that the eyes of the entire world are upon it today. . . .[37]

In other words, the society of the present was thoroughly unsatisfactory and must be transformed. And while Italy had given fascism to the world, unfortunately fascism was still incomplete. Until Italian fascism has been brought to fruition, the crisis of the Western world would not be resolved. Further, fascism would not be merely a technique for government or a

method of economic organization, but a new way of conceptu-
alizing life, a new approach to human problems:

> ... it is necessary to create a new spiritual climate in the shortest
> possible time. . . . Only when Italy has an intimate and profound
> culture, felt as a fascist culture, will we be able to say that the
> Revolution has been accomplished . . . actions are worth much
> but . . . it is always the idea which guides peoples and makes
> them civilized. . . .[38]

The fascism of the future, then, would involve a fundamental
change in the nature of human life. Not content with resolving
the contradictions inherent in the institutions of the modern
world, the young group at *La Sapienza* called for the restructuring of the human condition itself. As Spinetti put it in the
second issue of the journal: "[Fascism] wants to remake not the
forms of life, but the content, the man, the character, the
faith."[39]

The problem with all of this was that, by their own admission, fascists had not found the means for achieving such a
transformation. While they were unanimous in their cry for a
new order, a radical transformation of both the world and its
human inhabitants, they had no concrete alternative to propose,
nor were they altogether clear about the means for discover-
ing the new order. Where should they begin?

While the future might be clouded with uncertainties, it did
seem to Spinetti and his *confrères* that they knew where to
begin to look for the criteria on which the new world-view
would be based. The only element within modern society which
as yet had not been corrupted by the germs of the old order
was the youth which had come to age under the fascist regime.
Consequently that group, and that group alone, could provide
the impetus for the fascism of the future so ardently desired
and sought after.

As we have seen, this suggestion had been given public

support by Arnaldo Mussolini for quite some time, and it is no
accident that Spinetti was the editor of the first anthology of
Arnaldo's writings in 1936. The pages of *La Sapienza*, beginning with the first number, were filled with the pleas of young
fascists that their moment had arrived, and that it was high
time the old men of the regime made a serious attempt to draw
upon this source of genuine fascist inspiration. And such pleas
were not made only by those who were young themselves.
For example, Massimo Pallottino, a well-known Etruscologist,
put it this way in the first issue of *La Sapienza:*

> . . . It is time for the State . . . to make contact with this obscure
> and scattered work of thought, to guide its tendencies directly,
> eliminate its abuses, appraise and coordinate its best parts. . . .[40]

Behind the somewhat euphemistic language of this proposal
we can see the frustration of a member of a generation which
was not finding satisfactory outlets for its energies. Ironically,
a main complaint which the fascists of 1922 had directed
against *trasformismo* (the policies of Giolitti and his successors)
would now be directed against themselves: that the State had
become atrophied because its ranks were closed to new blood.

There was a further problem. As Spinetti observed in
February, 1933, it was often difficult to locate those members
of his generation who were most capable. Many of them did
not attend school, and even those who did were frequently
unknown to their teachers. Even if the State were to undertake
a massive program to integrate young people into the regime,
it would be in danger of failing to locate the best elements.
Spinetti therefore proposed that the government encourage
spontaneous youth gatherings, and the Anti-Idealist Convention
was to be one such meeting.

Just how spontaneous the Convention was, is very difficult to
judge. On the face of it, Spinetti and his friends seemed to be

taking a tremendous risk in organizing a public manifestation against the man judged by many to be the court philosopher of fascism. Not only did Gentile occupy the prestigious position of director of the Fascist Institute of Culture, but he had inaugurated the "most fascist reform" of the schools at the onset of Mussolini's regime. Gentile, furthermore, would collaborate with the Duce himself in the writing of the *Political Doctrine of Fascism* two years later for the *Encyclopedia*, a work under the general supervision of Gentile himself. It was then, it would seem, an act of considerable courage for young fascists to organize a demonstration against the apostle of Italian Idealism.

But the situation was not that simple, and Gentile had managed to antagonize more than Spinetti and the adherents of *fascismo universale*. Arrogant and indiscreet, he had let it be known for years that he considered opponents of his Idealist doctrines to be unreceptive to rational argument and therefore adherents of outmoded philosophical positions.[41] This position, irritating enough when directed against lay thinkers, bordered on heresy when directed against the clergy, and Gentile on at least two occasions had enraged his clerical opponents.

In March, 1930, he had given a lecture at the University of Bologna, having been invited there by followers associated with the journal *Vita Nova*. In his speech entitled "*Stato e cultura*" (State and Culture), Gentile repeated his usual claim that his system was the only true interpretation of fascism. Then, in responding to criticism from Cardinal Nasalli Rocca, he launched a diatribe not only against philosophical and cultural doctrines differing from his own, but also against the Pope himself. According to a letter received by Mussolini on March 14, Gentile had proclaimed the Pope incapable of comprehending pure, Idealistic philosophy and called him the *maestro* only of Thomism and of conceptions which verged on materialism![42]

Just how long it took the Church to react is hard to say, but its formal action took place early in 1934, when Gentile was condemned along with Benedetto Croce, a condemnation which was viewed with considerable alarm by many fascists.[43] Their fear was that the attack upon Gentile might well be construed as an attack upon fascism itself. Indeed, there is some evidence that many Catholics reacted in exactly this way. In the letter to Mussolini describing the reaction to the condemnation, the Duce's informant refers to yet another harsh polemic between Gentile and members of the clergy, in particular with Father Gemelli, the rector of the Catholic University of Milan.[44]

In short, during a period when Mussolini was attempting to smooth out the relations between the Vatican and his own regime, Gentile was busily going about Italy incurring the collective wrath of the Italian clergy, even attacking the Pope himself. In 1936 the situation had reached such a point that Gentile was removed from his position at the *Scuola Normale Superiore* of Pisa. There is some evidence that this was done without the authorization of the Duce. Mussolini remarked that "the understanding was that actions would be taken if Senator Gentile continued in his polemical attacks. And the Senator, after my warning, cut off the polemic. . . ."[45] Yet Mussolini's warning, and his conditional instruction that Gentile was to be removed from the School at Pisa, are clearly indicative of Gentile's tenuous standing in the regime.

Given all this, the very least that can be said is that Gentile's position within the fascist hierarchy was far from unassailable. Indeed, one who attacked Gentile could count, at worst, upon a certain degree of support from clerical ranks. In the light of this evidence, the criticism from Spinetti and his associates at *La Sapienza* does not necessarily look like an act of intellectual courage. Indeed, it might well be that Mussolini observed such a demonstration with some pleasure, for it helped insulate him from the charge that Gentile spoke for fascism.

Further, had Spinetti's actions been such as to antagonize the
fascist hierarchs, it is unlikely that he would have enjoyed the
success he found thereafter within fascist ranks. Yet shortly after
the Anti-Idealist Convention, he was invited to join the staff of
Popolo d'Italia, and he continued to find employment throughout the regime's duration. His activities, moreover, continued
along the same lines, and his ideological views were to alter
little, if at all, in the years after 1933.

Rather than undergoing any substantial modifications, Spinetti's ideas regarding the role of youth in the coming fascist
transformation were reinforced by his experiences during Mussolini's regime. In 1940 he was asked to report to the Minister
of Popular Culture on the first national conference of the School
of Fascist Mysticism in Milan. Spinetti was of course highly
sympathetic to the entire enterprise, and his lengthy report to
Minculpop deserves substantial consideration.[46]

He began by noting that the persons at the conference could
be divided into three groups: *squadristi* and veterans of the
Great War; older men and university professors; and youths
and veterans of the African and Spanish campaigns. Each of
these groups, according to Spinetti, held distinct views both on
the role of the School of Fascist Mysticism and of youth in
fascist society.

The *squadristi* and veterans of the First World War were
highly belligerent, typically pounded their fists on the table
when they spoke, and called for severe discipline of the sort
they had shown in their past glories. They suggested that true
mysticism called for a rigid obedience to the will of Mussolini,
which was never to be questioned.

The professors and other elderly people were generally
sceptical of the enterprise itself.

The young people, on the other hand, while lacking the clear
principles of the veterans and older men, were in total agree-

ment on two broad points. The first was that it was absurd to
call for faith in doctrines which could not be discussed or
questioned, let alone to call for action based on this "faith."
The second was that the bases for future action had to be discussed and challenged, because they all felt the need for "a new
synthesis" and were certain that they were capable of constructing it." Spinetti went on to elaborate this theme, a theme which
he had himself voiced many times in the past:

> . . . the young people showed themselves to be dissatisfied both
> with the accommodating or sceptical themes of the elderly and
> the professors, and with the affirmations, full of faith but ration-
> ally undemonstrable, of the *squadristi* and the veterans of the
> Great War. . . .
> . . . they applauded all those who extended them an invitation to
> construct and not to act and obey passively. . . .[47]

This report is significant for a variety of reasons. First, it
shows the ability of an individual like Spinetti to maintain a
critical position throughout the *Ventennio*. Second, it documents the signal failure of the regime to integrate young people
into the system, an integration which was fervently desired by
the fascist hierarchs. As late as 1940, in an institution designed
to encourage a spirited participation in the cultural life of the
nation, there was still a clear dissatisfaction with fascist ideology
and fascist culture.

It seems that such youth would be naturally anti-fascist, or,
at the very least, anti-Mussolini. Yet this was not often the case.
Despite the failure of the regime to attract such youth enthusiastically to the fascist banner, they insisted upon dedication to a
fascism which as yet no one had elaborated. Once having found
it, their obedience would be unquestioned. While such young
fascists might become genuine anti-fascists later on, for the
most part they simply demanded the right to participate in the
elaboration of the new system. Spinetti, whose critical position

has been amply demonstrated, was adamant in his call for self-discipline, for a dedicated obedience to those principles which *had* been elucidated.

In 1936, Spinetti published a book entitled *L'Europa verso la Rivoluzione* (*Europe Towards the Revolution*). Beginning with the by-now familiar claim that the Western world was convulsed by a crisis "of the system . . . a crisis of civilization," Spinetti announced that the Fascist Revolution was ". . . the expression of that anti-individualistic conscience which must produce the new civilization in short order."[48] He continued by pointing to the facts of human nature upon which a fascist conception of the State rested. Man is, by his very essence, driven to discover his own nature, and in that act of self-discovery obtains control over himself. The man who is most completely aware of himself and his own potentialities is simultaneously the man who can most effectively control and discipline himself. Since man can only achieve liberty by the full actualization of his own essence, it follows that liberty equals discipline.

The crisis which Spinetti saw convulsing Western society was essentially a crisis of the spirit, a crisis which would destroy the individualistic preconceptions of the old liberal world. Whereas liberalism and Bolshevism both started with society and derived human nature from social conditions, fascism was unique in that it had developed a social theory from a new cognizance of the essence of man. As such, only fascism provided a means of resolving the contemporary crisis. To deal with the crisis of the twentieth century, man had to abandon the individualistic concepts on which he had based his previous existence and enter into a new collectivity. "The moral greatness of a man—as of a people—is in direct relation to the sacrifices he is prepared to make."[49]

While this sort of statement is always made by those who seek to enlist national energies in a war effort, it is also consistent with everything Spinetti had to say on the subject both before and after the Ethiopian War. Further, while calling for discipline and engagement in the war in Ethiopia, Spinetti also called for increased dedication to the elaboration of the principles on which the new order was to be based.

Six years later we find the same themes appearing in his last work during the fascist period, *Fascismo e Libertà* (*Fascism and Liberty*, 1941). Significantly subtitled "Towards a New Synthesis," the work reiterated the fundamental notion of Spinetti's world-view: that youth was uniquely equipped to provide a new system of thought for a world in desperate need of a guide for its actions. This new doctrine would be of self-control and full self-consciousness; only such a doctrine could enable man to "enjoy true liberty, which to most people today appears unattainable."[50] These, according to Spinetti, were the fundamental insights of Mussolini, the insights upon which the elaboration of the new synthesis must be based.

The evidence for the truth of this claim for Spinetti lay in the kind of disjunction which he saw in the Western world between theory and practice. On all sides people's lives were demonstrably unrelated to their ideals. This could be seen in all fields of human activity, but most clearly in the area of culture, where the functions of the artist seemed almost totally unrelated to human aspirations:

> Today culture does not intimately explain life, religion does not rationally justify it, art inadequately represents it; in no field of human activity does one find a correspondence between intuition and expression, between thought and life.[51]

Such a bifurcation between thought and action derived from the same source as the crisis of the Western world: the endless and irresponsible pursuit of individual gain by members of society. The exigencies of the present situation did not permit such behavior, and that was the reason for Spinetti's definition of the crisis of the West as a moral crisis. It was therefore necessary to make people abandon the old ideology of individualism, and to do so in such a way that their energies were not stifled in a new bureaucratic system, but liberated and directed toward the service of the common good. The need was an urgent one, and the goal could be defined rather precisely:

> The [men of our time] do not simply desire to combat leveling collectivism and exasperated individualism, but intend to create a new system of thought which destroys individualism without eliminating individuality.[52]

By its very nature, a system of ideas which could provide this new synthesis was universally applicable and involved the resolution of religious as well as secular problems. For this reason any attempt to separate "political" from "religious" ideals would be necessarily lopsided and incomplete. Yet the old syntheses, above all the Idealistic attempts, had been lopsided themselves. It seemed that those who had grown up under the old order were incapable of producing a new mode of thinking, and once again Spinetti returned to his fundamental theme: the new doctrine must come from the new man, the generation raised in the fascist milieu.

> The new man . . . must act in such a way that the idea of a superior perfection triumphs over contingent necessity and brutish instincts; he must recognize and actualize the final order of values, his own true nature.[53]

The implication of Spinetti's writings is that the old generation must learn from the youth of the nation. Rather than the traditional relationship between the generations, Spinetti advocated a reversal of their roles. In this, he was doing more than merely elaborating the belief of Arnaldo Mussolini that the young would be better than the fascists of the first hour; he was calling for a group of people in power to permit some of those they governed to become the educators of the nation. But for that to happen, the government had to be willing to tolerate a tremendous amount of criticism and, in Spinetti's words of 1933, many spontaneous demonstrations.

Remarkably enough, it seems that much of this freedom of expression was available to the younger generation. While control of the daily press had been well established in 1934 and 1935, and was extended even further through the establishment of the Ministry of Popular Culture in 1937, a system of censorship was not rigorously applied to youth periodicals. Testimony to this curious state of affairs comes not only from Spinetti but also from Ruggero Zangrandi.[54] Further, examination of the sort of literature common to many youth groups during the *Ventennio* supports this conclusion.

Zangrandi has written about some of these groups, and again and again reports that many of them—including some that were extremely outspoken against various elements of the regime— were subsidized by the Party, or even by the Ministry of Popular Culture. Zangrandi himself, often the author of remarks highly critical of fascist practice, was employed by *Popolo d'Italia*. In addition, he has reported some striking cases, such as that of Mario La Rosa, who had incurred the wrath of many of the most important fascist leaders by writing a highly critical exposé of Sicilian landed estates. La Rosa was subsequently given financial support by the Ministry of Popular Culture, and was put in charge of a journalistic agency concerned with Italian youth.

Spinetti's own case is no less remarkable. As editor of *La Sapienza* he had been highly outspoken in his remarks about the unsatisfactory nature of the hierarchs of fascism, yet he was invited to participate in the Press Bureau, and then helped to edit *Popolo d'Italia*. Later, as we have seen, he too was employed by the Ministry of Popular Culture.

What is so striking about this testimony is that it corresponds so well with the ideological treatment of Italian youth. Not only was youth given an exalted position in the rhetoric of fascism, not only was it encouraged to strike out on new ideological paths, but the experimentation and the criticism of the status quo which such experiments entailed were tolerated by the regime.

It would seem, then, that Spinetti's own summary is a fair one, that "under fascism one could write what one wanted, using standard catchwords, especially on the part of youth, whom Mussolini assumed to be in good faith."[55] Spinetti felt that the regime was much more concerned with the censorship of obscene and lascivious material in fascist youth journals than with the suppression of their political criticism.

Two observations seem in order here. First, the tactic of inviting some of the more provocative journalists to join in the literary enterprises of the fascist "establishment" is not necessarily evidence of a high degree of literary freedom. Indeed, it might well be viewed as a form of what today we term "co-opting" critics of the regime. By involving them in the journalistic institutions of the dictatorship, it may well have been easier to control their critical writings. Yet had this been the case it is difficult to account for the continued criticism from a figure like Spinetti. It seems, instead, that the segment of the press directed toward fascist youth enjoyed a considerable autonomy. Which brings us to the second point: these opportunities for self-expression did not extend to publications from other segments of the literary community.

> The young, in other words, felt themselves freer than their elders in sustaining their own ideas, both because their criticisms were tolerated more than those of the older people, and because in criticizing fascism they did not, like their elders, refer to their past. . . .[56]

The immediate result of this toleration goes far toward explaining the attitudes of many who might otherwise have turned to the anti-fascist groups in the thirties. Given the toleration of various attitudes within fascism itself, criticism of the regime could take place within a "fascist" framework, and was not driven to explicitly anti-fascist manifestations. To put it in different terms: the problem of anti-fascism was not operative for many young intellectuals, since they were concerned with, and were able to work for, a change *within* fascism itself.

Here we must make a distinction between the kind of "loyal opposition" to fascism which characterized many of the young intellectuals along with figures like Bottai and his followers, and the genuine anti-fascist activities of Carlo and Nello Rosselli and the "*Guistizia e Libertà*" (Justice and Liberty) movement. Out-and-out enemies of fascism could clearly not be seduced into believing that any substantive change within a fascist framework would produce an acceptable Italian society. They had seen the oppressive nature of fascism, were convinced that Mussolini was to be opposed at all costs, and fought for the destruction of fascism, not its transformation. While there was more of this sort of activity in Italy than in other fascist countries, such courageous actions were not very widespread, especially among the young members of a fascist generation who had been guaranteed a major role in shaping the destiny of Italy (and indeed of Western civilization).

It is difficult indeed for any citizen to come to the conclusion that his own country has become a menace to human progress and humane society, and even when one suspects that his government is behaving terribly, the commitments to national tradition, family, and friends are very potent ones. A more common response than total rupture with one's native land is to demand that the government be reformed. And when one is convinced that such reform is possible, and indeed that it is imminent, awaiting only one's own efforts to guarantee success, open revolt becomes highly problematical.

Many young fascist intellectuals were deeply dissatisfied with their government, yet failed to make the kind of clean break which the Rossellis were able to achieve. These young fascists believed that they would be able to correct fascism's errors and enhance its merits, and they did not think that they lived under a repressive regime. Were they not, after all, permitted to criticize? Were not their words echoed by Mussolini himself? They did not see what Rosselli and others had seen, the suppression of any meaningful freedom of press and speech. Rather, they saw in their own circumstances a considerable amount of freedom, and they were lured on by the prospect of assuming the guidance of Italy themselves.

Much of the thinking and writing on the part of young fascist intellectuals was challenging and original, and attracted a considerable amount of sympathy from some important fascist leaders, like Giuseppe Bottai and Arnaldo Mussolini. If suppression of the pre-fascist press was virtually complete, there was nonetheless a wide range of ideas and attitudes which emerged in publications that the regime judged "loyal." Paramount among these were those journals written by young fascists themselves.

Such a view seems justified by the wide variety of youth publications which appeared during the *Ventennio*, especially in the period 1930–35. One of the most stimulating and impressive of these was *L'Universale*, in Florence.

The importance of this journal was illustrated recently by the appearance of an anthology of the more significant articles published during its brief life. Its brilliant editor, Berto Ricci, was killed in Libya in 1941 at the age of thirty-six, and may serve as an example of the sort of enthusiasm and independence possessed by many young fascist thinkers. His journal, as he told the readers of its first number in January, 1931, was intended to play a major role in Italian life and society. Its foundation was intended to demonstrate his generation's determination "to act upon the history of Italy." Typically enough, Ricci took care to distinguish between what counted in "history" and what was trivial in human affairs: "Not everything is history: history is not that which passes, it is that which endures. . . ."[57]

In impassioned tones reminiscent of the great nineteenth-century nationalist Giosuè Carducci at his best, Berto Ricci called for a Renaissance of Italian culture. "We learned to write from Niccolò Machiavelli and from the people of the Oltrarno, who are thus our most direct masters. Whoever believes that they have created us is deceived. . . ."[58] Ricci and his group considered themselves independent of the "masters" of the day, and proposed the formation of an intellectual élite, an élite of those few who were capable of contributing to the culture of civilized men.

The particular sort of civilization they sought to create was not to be tied to any of the illusions of modern man. Most particularly, this new order had to be freed from the prejudices of their contemporaries. Thus, undoubtedly with an eye to the more hypernationalistic outcries of the vitriolic *squadristi*, Ricci announced that much of what he and his friends proposed would "be distasteful to many, and make many laugh." He then spelled out the illusions he had rejected:

> We will be . . . universal, and against any residue of nationalism; modern, and without idols . . . we will be hot, which is the way of men. It behooves our century to bring back to the Italian mentality the mantle of vastness, love and ardor, the domination over times and nations. . . .[59]

The universality of the new mentality was a natural out-growth of the universal crisis of the twentieth century. As Ricci surveyed the situation, he, like Spinetti (and like Mussolini) saw a crisis which threatened all major institutions and convictions of the past. All areas of human thought and endeavor were falling into decadence and atrophy: "the decadence of Western civilization in its nationalist and capitalist aspects, as well as in its most ancient and solemn one, Christianity."[60]

Ricci went on to analyze this triple catastrophe. Nationalism was no longer the vehicle for the expression of the general will, and indeed in modern Europe it often functioned as a mask, concealing the desires of private elements. Conflicts between such private components contrasted sharply with the growing universalism of ideas and habits throughout the West, and these newer habits provided the basis for a new order of civilization.[61]

The degeneration of capitalism hardly needed documentation in 1931. Indeed, one would be hardpressed to find enthusiastic defenders of the capitalistic system in that year of depression and worldwide anxiety. It was a time when fascist proposals for a Corporate State were receiving serious consideration all over the West. That the final structure of this Corporatism was the subject of a heated debate within Italy itself was no obstacle to such consideration, and indeed it seemed possible that some such solution would have to be applied on a worldwide scale.

Finally, it seemed to Ricci that Christianity itself was exhausted as a religious ideology, and he foresaw a future in which Italy would become a secular society, abandoning her confessional tradition: ". . . our civil tradition will not re-enter the Catholic one and can and has been able to develop independently of it. . . ."[62]

The crisis, then, was seen to have affected all the major areas of Western civilization. Ricci here stands together with Spinetti and Arnaldo and Benito Mussolini. The major innovation in Ricci's analysis—and it is a crucial distinction—is that the

Christian tradition has become irrelevant. Both Arnaldo Mussolini and Spinetti had insisted that the future development of
fascism would take place within an essentially Christian framework, and the rhetoric of fascism was unequivocal on the subject. Again and again Mussolini reminded his audiences, both in
Italy and abroad, that the Rome of fascism was heir to the
traditions of both the Roman Empire and the Rome upon which
the Catholic Church rested. Depending upon the setting, the
Duce would claim that Rome had emerged to save the Western
world for a third or fourth time—the extra act of salvation
being the Renaissance.[63] Yet Ricci, the Tuscan iconoclast, broke
with this tradition as well.

For Ricci, the Western world had attempted two cures of its
fatal malady during its twentieth-century death spasms: Russian
Bolshevism and Indian Gandhiism. The first was viewed as
simply the Russian destruction of a dying feudal structure, while
the second, for all its genius, was unique to India and unsuitable
for application in other societies. However, Ricci was willing to
entertain the possibility that both these movements might con-
ceivably have a role to play within the framework of the new
order; an order which was to embrace every race and every
country. The energies which Lenin and Gandhi had unleashed
in the world would play a contributory role in the new civilization. The leadership of that new order would, however, be
Italian, since Italy was the one country capable of carrying out
the original universal mission of the Roman Empire: that of
civilizing the entire world.[64]

In these terms, Ricci and his young colleagues at *L'Universale*
called for the formation of a new empire, based not upon
military conquest, but rather upon Italy's unique capacity for
civilization: "Attila and Tamerlane could not found empires.
[We] believe, with Dante, that this task awaits Italy and Rome,
and [we] believe that the empires of the others are merely
echoes and shadows of it."[65]

The grounds upon which this grandiose claim was based are now familiar to us. Italy alone, it was argued, possessed the creative genius which must perforce lie at the heart of the new world. Not material wealth, nor strength of armies, nor magnitude of production, but greatness of spirit was called for in the new civilization. This new civilization was thus linked to the cosmic visions of two of Italy's greatest messianic prophets:

> [We] see in the Italian revolution an undertaking in progress for liberty and national unity, now carried to the highest level and made a people and an impulse on the European plane, making fascism the necessary premise for the human Empire which will embody the Monarchy of Dante and the Council of Mazzini. . . .[66]

This, then, was the role that Berto Ricci and his Florentine friends had designed for themselves in the coming Fascist Revolution. They, as young intellectuals unsullied by the corruptions of the present, were to make history in the fullest possible meaning of that phrase. They intended to develop the traditions of their country and their civilization in such a way as to make them the basic tenets of a new order in the world. But the nature of the new civilization would have little in common with those principles which had been taken as the backbone of traditional Western culture, and consequently the first act of the Revolution would be to sweep the refuse of the present into the garbage bin of history: "[we] believe therefore that it is a grave error to define fascism as the saviour of Western civilization, rather than coming to kill it. . . ."[67]

Clearly, the act of destruction which would precede the flowering of the new fascist hegemony would sweep away the present generation of Italians, along with the rest of the dross of "Western civilization." But the new culture, as always, remained to be elaborated. The renaissance of Italian genius would lay the basis for the new fascist Empire. So, for all its universal goals and international rhetoric, *L'Universale* concentrated the bulk of its energies on the one clear task immediately at hand: the development of *Italian* culture.

This was true as well of the Roman journal *Il Saggiatore*, under the direction of Domenico Carella and Giorgio Granata. Appearing for the first time in April, 1930, and for the last in December, 1933, *Il Saggiatore* was dedicated to the clarification of the ideas at work among the members of the new generation of Italian youth, and to the elucidation of the new culture. To this end the first issue was devoted to an analysis of the new generation, and included comments by such luminaries as Paolo Orano, Margherita Sarfatti, Ugo D'Andrea, F. T. Marinetti, and Ugo Betti.[68]

The conclusions reached by the Romans were markedly similar to those of the Florentines we have already examined. Italy, the Romans concluded, was in a period of great crisis, equivalent to the crisis which preceded the emergence of Christianity in the ancient world. And just as that ancient convulsion had given a new spirit to the West, so the present time of troubles would reshape the mentality of Western man. This was felt most intensely by the literate youth of Italy, who were confident that they were living in a period between two historical epochs, and that their duty was to shape the new world.

The willingness of so many leading fascist intellectuals to contribute to an investigation of Italy's youth shows both the importance of the issue and the seriousness of youthful enterprise under the regime. It is significant that the intellectuals solicited by *Il Saggiatore* came largely from two main intellectual currents: futurism and the corporatist doctrines associated with Giuseppe Bottai. Further, the inclusion of Margherita Sarfatti, the mistress of Mussolini, suggests that the dictator himself was not unconcerned with this theme.

The conviction that the present lay between two distinct and greatly different periods of world history, and that the younger generation would be the group to bridge the gulf between these two eras, was common enough; not only was it a fundamental notion of virtually all the groups of young intellectuals we have discussed, but it had been stated explicitly by Mussolini in the Piazza Venezia on October 16, 1932 ("We stand before a transition from one epoch of civilization to another").

Such problems were very real to Italian fascists, as indeed they were to European fascists in general. The directors of *Il Saggiatore* did not equivocate in the least. The present generation of Italian youth, they said, felt themselves standing at the beginning of a new epoch and were intolerant of "every rhetorical form empty of concrete significance, of all those institutions which today are only a conservative obstacle to contemporary life."[69] What did they offer instead? Although they were themselves the authors of a good deal of the empty rhetorical forms they condemned in their elders' writings, the young theorists had a significant notion of the future. Somewhat vaguely at first, but with increasing clarity, they called for the creation of a new kind of human being, a new man who would remake the world. A change in institutions is worthless without a change in men, and since the institutions of the world are crashing down on all sides, men must be changed. "In the face of these transformations man must also work a revolution within himself. . . ."[70]

Here the ideas of *Il Saggiatore*'s writers again joined with Spinetti and the rhetoric of Mussolini. In the search for the universal relevance of fascism, the Duce had argued that fascism was far more than a mere change in government, than a substitution of a new set of institutions for the old ones. Predictably, the notion of the "new fascist man" was elevated to the status of holy writ. Its *locus classicus* is the "official" history of fascism written by Gioacchino Volpe in 1936:

> In the new concept that fascism has of Italians there is outlined a new concept of man, a concept of him as he should be according to civilized ideas; as culture united with action and almost

identical with action, as instruction equal to education, as science that does not diffuse itself in abstract knowledge but [acts] as a conscious force for elucidating all in life and all for life; as a dynamic spirit of realization. . . .[71]

The concept of the "new man" who would establish fascism once and for all was not restricted to the Italian milieu. It is, indeed, common to all of European fascism.[72] Implicit or explicit in the writings of virtually all the youth groups we have discussed, it was an intellectual weapon which cut not only against the nonfascist societies of Europe, but also with equal keenness against a generation which had grown old in power in Rome. The adoption of this concept by Mussolini demonstrates the commitment of the regime to taking on at least the trappings of a profound change in the early 1930's, as its enthusiastic promulgation by Italian youth shows their desire for such a change.

Thus, at the highest level, the ideals of recalcitrant young intellectuals flowed together with official doctrine. It is important to note that this emphasis upon the universality of fascist doctrine represented a major departure from previous pronouncements. In fact the *volte-face* on the part of the regime was so substantial that Mussolini was finally forced to make a public repudiation of his own previous views. "The phrase 'Fascism is not merchandise for export' is not mine," he announced, "it is too banal . . ."[73]

The banality was too great for a growing element within Italy which demanded recognition of a larger sphere of fascist application. Many young fascists could publicly use these ideas to bolster their own positions *vis-à-vis* various members of the hierarchy who clung to more nationalistic views and could also expand their own sphere of activity beyond the purely national context onto a European plane.

While this debate was taking place within Italian circles, it had already made itself felt internationally. The initial public proposal that fascism should play a universal role in the West had come from an Italian living in England, Camillo Pellizzi, in 1925, and various groups throughout Europe were committed to this doctrine. When Mussolini gave it official recognition in 1930, young Italians would find substantial support for their ideas all over the continent.

The elevation of the doctrine to the status of orthodoxy was completed on October 27, 1930, when Mussolini announced:

> Today I affirm that Fascism, as idea, doctrine, and realization, is universal: Italian in its particular institutions, and universal in spirit.[74]

The curious history of *fascismo universale* properly begins on that date.

CHAPTER THREE

Towards the International

/.V.V.\ The idea of a universal fascism destined to transform the face of the European continent developed at a time when Mussolini was looking beyond the domestic boundaries of his Fascist Regime for new projects and adventures. The consolidation of the regime was achieved in the late twenties, and the thirties were above all the era of the fascist "Empire." This momentous transformation reflected many of the changes which fascism had undergone during its first decade in power, profound changes which must be analyzed before the full significance of projects for a Fascist International can be understood.

Unlike the Nazis, whose achievement of a monolithic State entailed the expansion and consolidation of the Nazi Party, Mussolini's dictatorship was a uniquely personal one, and was largely achieved *at the expense* of the *Partito Nazionale Fascista*. Beginning with the Matteotti crisis in 1924, Mussolini worked throughout the twenties first to discipline and then to disarm the Party. This was accomplished during the tenure of Augusto Turati as Secretary of the Party; by 1928 the PNF, which had been able to dictate to Mussolini in the early twenties, was essentially reduced to the status of an extension of the governmental bureaucracy. In keeping with the slogan "Everything in the State, nothing outside the State, nothing against the State," the discipline and capture of the Party was a necessary step in the construction of the new Fascist State. The success of this enterprise meant that Mussolini need no longer fear the menace of the kind of *ultimata* which had harassed him so frequently in the first three years of his rule.[1]

As the Party was being brought under governmental control, Mussolini extended the sphere of his discipline to other areas of Italian political activity. The crushing of the traditional political parties was facilitated by the fatuous opposition movement of the Aventine Succession of 1924,[2] which drove the more liberal parliamentary elements far outside any effective sphere of legislative action, and left Mussolini with a free hand to reorganize the legislature itself. By the end of the decade the Fascist Party was the only legally recognized political party, and control over its membership was strictly exercised by the Secretary, who in turn had taken his place in the governmental structure. Further, the reorganization of the legislature and the change in the electoral laws which were promulgated in 1928 gave the Grand Council of Fascism (a governmental rather than a Party organization) virtually complete control of the selection of candidates for the new House. With the passage of time, the Grand Council itself became increasingly the right arm of the dictator and its meetings became significantly ever less frequent.[3]

In short, the first decade of fascist rule had produced a unique personal dictatorship, which left Mussolini with no single opponent in the political realm capable of opposing his will. The emasculation of the old parties, the transformation of the legislature, the "purification" of the Fascist Party itself, and the isolation of the monarchy from any effective role in decision making, all combined to ensure the widest possible scope for Mussolini's initiative. At the same time, the dictator had acted to reduce the effectiveness of the two large organizations from the economic sector, the *Confindustria* on the side of the businessmen, and the *Confederazione di Sindacati Fascisti* (Confederation of Fascist Trade Unions) on the side of the workers.[4]

The discipline of the economic organizations was as necessary to Mussolini as that of the political structures, and his actions in the twenties went hand in hand with his strokes against his potential political foes. As Renzo De Felice has recently demonstrated, fascist economic policy in the twenties—in particular the deflationary actions taken between 1925 and 1927, and the revaluation of the lira at the level of the famous "quota 90"— must be viewed as actions designed to drive the industrialists into the arms of the Duce.[5] The harshness of the revaluation was designed to demonstrate to the business leaders the absolute indispensability of Mussolini himself, and also the force of his own will in formulating economic policy. Having beaten them with the stick of deflation and revaluation, Mussolini was then able to turn around and offer them the carrot of guarantees against strikes by their class enemy.

In endearing himself to the industrialists by guaranteeing the continual operation of their factories and promising State intervention against strikers, Mussolini simultaneously struck a blow at one of the few organizations which might have been capable of posing a counterforce to his own strength. Edmundo Rossoni's Confederation of Fascist Trade Unions was the only surviving organization in Italy which could pretend to some sort of radical intent.[6] The Fascist Party, originally populated by the *enragé* elements of Italian socialism, had long since abandoned any pretense of radical aim, but this tradition of fascist socialism was kept alive by Rossoni and his followers. The treatment of the Confederation by Mussolini was in keeping with his actions toward other strong groups; not only was the traditional proletarian weapon of the strike taken away from the workers, but the Confederation itself was dissolved into smaller units in keeping with the new "corporate" structure which was being introduced in the late twenties.[7]

Finally, the keystone in the triumphal arch of fascist consolidation was unquestionably the Conciliation with the Vatican, which not only gave Mussolini tremendous prestige both at home and abroad, but also acted to insulate fascism from some of the more pointed tongues in the Church.[8] The Church, too, became defused as a potentially explosive element in Italy.

The situation, then, as fascist Italy prepared to enter the 1930's was one of an effectively consolidated personal dictatorship, with potential enemies largely disarmed, co-opted, or driven into prison or exile. Control over the press was, legally at least, firmly established, and in terms of what we know about public opinion in the early and middle thirties, Mussolini's popularity would never again reach such heights.[9] Yet fascism seemed to many to be a failure, and Mussolini himself was well aware of the strong currents of discontent running through the country. We have already dealt with the important case of Giuseppe Bottai, and the significant elements of the youthful intelligentsia which followed the guiding genius of *Critica Fascista*. There were other voices, although many were not so outspoken as Bottai, suggesting that all was not right in the Palazzo Venezia. This is the origin of the oft-repeated rumor, which circulated among reputable fascist circles in the late twenties, that Mussolini had been "captured" by his entourage and become isolated from the "true fascists."[10]

This sort of complaint was tantamount to saying that the Fascist Revolution had been betrayed, and that the regime constructed with such terrible effort during the twenties was not "truly fascist." Since this complaint could hardly be voiced in Italy in the 1930's, it was translated into different terms. The context in which we encounter it most commonly is that of the "future of the Revolution," and all manner of opponents of the newly established regime were to be found under the generous folds of the revolutionary banner. Bottai, to take again one of the most important cases, put the question in its archetypal form on the first day of 1929: "Is the Revolution therefore completed? Is nothing left but to accept the closed cycle of its history as it exists in the institutes, the laws, the concretized regime?"[11] Bottai's own answer was that the Revolution was not complete but only begun, and that the major part of its creative activities lay ahead.

This conflict demonstrates the variegated nature of fascism. Mussolini's power rested upon a highly explosive coalition, and the volatility of this power base had already been demonstrated during the crisis of 1924. As the dictatorship grew more stable in the late twenties, many of the early leaders of fascism were disgruntled as they found themselves becoming less and less central to the affairs of the Italian State. Dissatisfaction with the nature of the regime was not by any means restricted to intellectuals like Bottai and his followers. Indeed, many of those who had participated in the early surge of squadrism were furious to find themselves occupying an ever more marginal position in fascist ranks, and the cries of betrayal directed at Mussolini came from various positions along the fascist spectrum.

What must be kept in mind throughout the period of the thirties is that critics of fascism within Italian society could have a variety of complaints about the structure of the regime, for the simple reason that the establishment of the Fascist State had been largely a haphazard operation. There was little about it which was intrinsically beyond modification. Mussolini had demonstrated his consummate ability to abandon allies and beliefs which had outlived their usefulness to him, and many fascists continued to support the regime in the belief that it was only a matter of time before they would win the Duce to their side. More often than not, those fascists who believed in a "revolutionary" fascism had come from syndicalist or anarcho-syndicalist ranks; and throughout the thirties they would attempt to convince Mussolini to re-embark upon the revolutionary path which, they thought, had characterized much of fascism in its heroic early days. Thus a man like Bottai could remain active in the Fascist Regime throughout the *Ventennio* in an attempt to revivify the potentially radical elements of the Corporatism for which he fought unsuccessfully in the late twenties. Innumerable other cases could be cited, but our concern here is more with a certain attitude of mind, a sort of self-hypnosis by which critics of the regime convinced themselves that fascism could change its direction, or, in the popular slogan, recapture the spirit of 1919.

If those who had fought and lost could remain on the field of battle, it is hardly surprising that many of the young Italians who came of age under fascism could believe that their battle, still to be waged, was destined to succeed. This belief was reinforced, as we have seen, by much of the rhetoric of fascist leaders as well as by that of Mussolini himself.

Furthermore, it is now possible to suggest that youth had a very real importance to Mussolini. The construction of the Fascist Regime had been accomplished at the expense of various groups within Italy, but rested upon no solid base. Diverse scholars have made this fundamental point,[12] but perhaps its classic statement was that of Stefano Jacini, shortly after the Second World War:

> The regime did not have at its disposal any compact group whose material and moral interests corresponded fully with its own, or were such as to tie it indissolubly to its wagon; to be sure, it theoretically dominated the entire nation, and actually availed itself here and there of devoted groups, and more frequently of influential persons; however neither the one nor the other normally represented the best, on the contrary they stood for the worst of the respective groups of origin.[13]

This situation arose logically out of the historical origins of the Fascist Regime itself. Having had to eliminate groups one at a time as potentially threatening to his own power, and indeed at times to his very continuation in office, Mussolini at the end found himself with no solid base of support. The much-vaunted ideology of the super-State which became codified in the thirties was in point of fact a reflection of fascism's failure to establish a solid base. The consequence of this was a frenetic search after "consensus," which masked the intrinsic weakness of fascism's political and social situation.

The implications of this instability are vital to an understanding of the importance of youth in the development of fascist practice and ideology in the period under consideration. Since the present generation of Italians had been eliminated from positions of influence and strength by Mussolini's maneuvers in the twenties, a genuine basis of loyalty and active support could not be expected for some time. We have seen the realization on the part of leading fascist hierarchs that the "fascistization" of the schools had been a failure, and it would be easy to cite similar failures in other important sectors of Italian life (most notably the working class).[14] What was crucial, however, was not the sense of failure surrounding a particular policy or group so much as a growing conviction on Mussolini's part that the entire generation which had marched on Rome was a failure. Thus Mussolini and many of the youthful critics of fascism were united in their condemnation of a particular generation in Italian history.

It is no accident that the calls for the revivification of fascism came from Arnaldo Mussolini and from the youthful sectors of the fascist intelligentsia. Arnaldo called for a generation which would not only follow his brother's will, but actually provide the kind of dynamic leadership for which Italians yearned so strongly. The young Italians, themselves committed to the heady goal of bringing the spirit of the *Risorgimento* back to Italian life, were the logical group in Italy for the kind of transformation the Duce was calling for. From Mussolini's point of view in the late twenties, all that was necessary was for the regime to endure, to survive. When the new generation came of age, it would provide the new blood which the aging body of Italian political and cultural life needed so desperately. We can find this theme as early as 1926, in one of Mussolini's speeches from the balcony of the Palazzo Venezia:

> My word of command is a verb: endure! Endure day by day, month by month, year by year, so that all the doubts, the criticisms, the opposition, smash themselves like dirt against the monolithic block of fascist will and tenacity.[15]

The prospect for the emergence of a new élite from the ranks of the young fitted neatly with the current rhetoric announcing the opening of a "new cycle" of fascism, and this kind of appeal made it possible to enlist many who had become disenchanted with the construction of the Fascist State itself. People who had been shunted out of the centers of power might now look forward to a new fascist epoch, as a time when their ideas could finally have a creative effect on history. There was therefore a twofold component to the demand that a new ruling class be created in Italy: a rejection of the limitations of fascism as then constituted, and a desire to reconsider some of the fundamental tenets upon which the regime apparently rested. Perhaps the clearest statement of the state of mind which characterized many of fascism's disillusioned followers was made by Giuseppe Bottai on the front page of *Critica Fascista* on June 15, 1930:

> . . . we might say that this appears to be the *conclusive* year for the work of constructing fascism. Having conquered the discipline of the Nation and the entire Italian people, which lives in a profoundly changed moral and historic climate, having ensured and restored to health the bases of the economy, reorganized the entire structure of the State, and regulated the pro-

ductive enterprise with the corporate order, the nearly eight years
achieved by fascism represent a titanic effort of will crowned
by full and undeniable success.

But the fact that we have reached all the objectives we proposed, far from meaning that fascism has exhausted its task,
obliges us to clarify from now on the new paths which still remain to be trodden. . . .[16]

Coming from Bottai, there is a peculiar irony to these words.
He was, after all, Minister of Corporations, the director of the
edifice which was supposed to be the masterpiece of fascist
theory: the corporate structures. But Bottai too had had some
of his sharper corporate teeth drawn, or at least filed down, by
Mussolini,[17] and the much-heralded Corporate State would
remain largely an interesting theory for academics and foreign
leaders. What is important here is the tone of frustration which
characterized Bottai's call for a continuing Revolution and, as
we shall see, the transformation of this frustration into a demand
for the expansion of fascism.

Having lauded the accomplishments of the regime, Bottai
turned to a prospectus for the future:

A movement of such vastness and scope as our own cannot
permit itself the luxury of easy dreams of past conquests . . .
since there must be a vigilant and constant effort to perfect and
adapt to a reality in constant change; but not even this most
delicate task, which employs all the tenacity we can muster, can
exempt us from the historic destiny of all great revolutions:
expansion beyond the limits of its own territory of birth and experiment. . . .[18]

With this, Bottai shifted the emphasis of his search to transform fascism onto an international plane. And here his ideas
corresponded fully with those of Mussolini, of many leading
fascists both at home and abroad, and above all of a highly
vocal and literate segment of Italian youth—to see the emergence of a universal fascism from the experimentation of the

twenties. For Mussolini, this was the result of the logic of his own regime. The general frustration and awareness that much of fascist "theory" remained on paper could not help but alarm the Duce, whose personal prestige and glory were at stake in the popularity of his regime. De Felice has described his reaction to the crisis of confidence as follows:

> . . . in the thirties Mussolini—seeing the "social" card of corporativism irremediably devalued in his hand—would end by searching for the "historic" justification of his power and by launching his regime anew by taking the route of all modern dictators, that of national "grandeur" and "strength," of colonial expansionism and military adventures.[19]

At first at least this policy met with considerable success. The period of the early thirties—until the beginning of the alliance with Hitler and the dreadful adventure in Spain—was the time of fascism's greatest popularity among the Italian people.[20] A large part of this popularity was due to the exciting prospect of seeing fascism become the model for the future of Europe, and—for those who had still not been disillusioned by the dictator's personal manipulation of his potential enemies— the prospect of developing something radically new and durable within the framework of fascism itself.

This scheme of launching a "new wave" of fascism on an international level also appealed to many who had been out- flanked by Mussolini in the first tests of strength in the twenties. Having lost the first round, they could still hope to emerge victorious in structuring fascism's international incarnation. Bot- tai seems to have been one such, for his enthusiastic adherence to the plan for the construction of a fascism which would be "merchandise for export" is otherwise very hard to explain. In fact, he had opposed the idea when it was first voiced in 1925 by Camillo Pellizzi. In a celebrated letter to *L'Epoca* in February, Pellizzi had sarcastically noted that only those Italians living outside the peninsula had been able to recognize that fascism had universal implications:

> That at last even our Roman leaders realize that there can be a universal sense and a universal function to fascism, is something destined to make us exiles happy, we advanced sentinels who have felt this truth almost like an epidermic sensation and have tried to spread this truth among our comrades for months and years. . . .[21]

In 1925 Bottai felt that it was inappropriate for the regime to dissipate its energies on such prospective developments as foreign "fascist" movements, and urged his followers not to become deflected from the main task before them: the construction of the Fascist State in Italy.[22] What had happened between 1925 and 1930 was that people like Bottai had lost any real hope for the achievement of their domestic programs, and consequently hoped the "exportation" of fascism might offer them some chance of bringing about the changes they desired.

By 1933 Bottai had come to agree with Pellizzi on the urgency of developing a coherent fascist doctrine which could be applied outside the Italian sphere. The terms in which Pellizzi described this new doctrine are of great interest to us, since they point both to the shortcomings of Italian fascism and to the failure of the regime to establish coherent centers of propaganda abroad. Pellizzi observed[23] that most of the propaganda abroad was centered on the person and speeches of Mussolini himself, and that the whole notion of the Fascist Revolution was therefore shrouded in mystery. Nobody seemed to know exactly what fascism represented, and for that reason it was foolhardy to presume that a worldwide adherence to it would spring up spontaneously.

He continued by making some serious observations on the shortcomings of fascist doctrine, in particular, the notion of Corporativism:

. . . Corporativism, naturally, is not what it should be, because it is still being made. Until it is something living, it will continue to create itself, and therefore will not be what it should. But it is time now that we stipulate what it *should be* . . . the Labor Charter is an important document, and it has been appreciated abroad; but in some measure the facts have already contradicted it, in part it has been surpassed, and there still exist (especially in the areas of principles and methods) vast zones of absolute obscurity. . . .[24]

The grounds for such a clarification were that without a coherent set of principles and formulas, fascism could not hope to be "exportable." This brings home one of the most interesting elements of the doctrine of universal fascism: it offered its supporters the opportunity to criticize fascism from the standpoint of the exigencies of a new international order, and thus served as a rallying point for many of the critics of the regime.

Aside from its domestic utility, the notion of universal fascism also had some serious pretensions on the international level. At the end of 1933 Pellizzi wrote a long letter to *Critica Fascista*,[25] complaining about the innumerable requests for information on fascism which were flooding his London mailbox, and observing that there was no single organization to which he could turn in an attempt to obtain such printed information. Instead, he was besieged by a long list of Italian organizations in England, asking him to speak, to write articles, or to provide information for their purposes. Noting that he was associated with the University of London, and not with either of the two traditional centers of English higher education, Pellizzi speculated that the Italians at Oxford and Cambridge must be inundated by such requests.

His complaint was a serious one, and points up the failure of the regime to organize its propaganda apparatus coherently. The large number of organizations which had entered the field of propaganda had produced chaos, and Pellizzi reasonably requested that the government take steps to centralize the entire operation.

Yet whatever the obstacles to the "exportation" of fascism, both Pellizzi and Bottai were agreed on its desirability by the middle thirties, and their enthusiastic support for the program of universal fascism shows the appeal of this ideology to fascists critical of many of the practices of the regime. After all, there was much in the rhetoric of Mussolini that could lead his followers to believe the new period of fascist expansion would entail a full-scale transformation of fascism itself. The "new cycle" of history which seemed to many to lie at hand might well provide dissident fascists with the opportunity to transform a regime which had become ossified. The question here is the amount of seriousness with which the regime, and Mussolini in particular, embarked upon the enterprise of spreading fascism onto a European plane. Was it simply a rhetorical flourish, or was there a substantial attempt to organize a practical fascist thrust on the Euopean scene? In analyzing this problem it is necessary to keep in mind the very close connection between domestic and foreign policy under Mussolini, for, as we have seen in other instances, the Duce's actions were motivated by a variety of concerns. Above all, he was desperately committed to the creation of a coherent and strictly organized fascist society at home, and his actions abroad must be viewed against that backdrop.

Most historians of the fascist period have concluded that the campaign for a worldwide fascist movement was a tactic by the dictator to extend his own prestige abroad while simultaneously enlarging his own domestic support.[26] This is undoubtedly true, yet the emphasis on the purely tactical nature of the program seems somewhat misplaced. The notion of universal fascism was, after all, closely tied to the concepts of Youth and national revivification already discussed at some length. Thus actions by

Mussolini, designed as they were to stimulate similar sympathies throughout the world, stemmed from a dynamic source within Italy itself. Indeed, it seems reasonable to suggest that Mussolini simply claimed for himself the sentiments of many fascist intellectuals, putting himself at the head of an already existent movement in order to expand both the boundaries and the anatomy of fascism.

By proclaiming his adherence to the principles of universal fascism, Mussolini was able to give many of his critics a new dedication to fascist Italy. As is often the case, however, the new rhetoric was not immediately followed by new actions, and Mussolini's problem became one of how to satisfy enhanced expectations. As we shall see, this was resolved, at least temporarily, by the call for the creation of a Fascist International, the Italian answer to international Bolshevism.

The transformation of fascism into a "universal" movement was immensely popular among youth, a popularity by no means restricted to the confines of the Italian peninsula. Enzo Santarelli has summarized the success of the "new face" of fascism:

> . . . fascism acquires a "universal" aspect, and appeals to the youth of Europe. All this explains sufficiently why the great mass of youth (save, perhaps, in the factories and at the level of a highly select intellectual élite) adheres to fascism.[27]

We must turn now to an examination of the doctrine itself, and shall begin by looking at perhaps the most widely read journals involved in the promulgation of *fascismo universale*, *Ottobre* and *Antieuropa* (*October* and *Anti-Europe*).

Ottobre, subtitled "The Journal of Universal Fascism," began its literary life on October 28, 1932, in Rome. Surely no fascist newspaper ever had a zodiacal pedigree as impressive as this one, and its title served to accentuate its appearance on the tenth anniversary of the March on Rome. Its director, Asvero

Gravelli, had an equally impressive fascist lineage. Gravelli was a member of the original *Fascio di Combattimento* in Milan, and participated in the celebrated sacking of the *Avanti* offices on April 15, 1919. He was involved in D'Annunzio's melodramatic storming of Fiume in 1919, and joined in numerous squadrist actions during the early twenties. He ultimately became one of the first leaders of the *Balilla* and served for a time as personal secretary to Michele Bianchi, one of the original quadrumvirs of fascism. With fascism installed in power, he turned his energies towards journalism, almost invariably aimed at the mobilization of youth. To this end, he founded *Giovinezza* and *La Giovane Italia*, two of the most important journals for young readers. In 1928 he founded the monthly journal *Antieuropa*, dedicated to the promulgation of the ideas of universal fascism, and the newspaper *Ottobre* served as its bi-weekly supplement. The title *Antieuropa* was designed to embody the hostility of the movement towards the "old Europe" of liberalism and capitalism. In February, 1934, *Ottobre* became a daily, testifying both to the popularity of its theme and to the financial support Gravelli was able to find for the enterprise.

Ottobre embodies all the basic themes of the universal fascism movement. Stressing the unity of the Fascist State, and its triumph in involving all classes in the State rather than constructing a rule on the power of one class, the contributors to *Ottobre* argued that fascism represented the only solution to the crises besetting the West. Its scope was never restricted to Italian problems, but stressed the universal applicability of fascist techniques. Thus, from its inception we find writers from all over Europe contributing to *Ottobre*. Further, considerable attention was devoted to the Nazi movement in Germany, and from the start *Ottobre* was unsparing in its criticism of the prophets of Nordic supremacy to the north. This concern with Hitler's movement would continue, as would the strident attacks on Nazi doctrine, particularly its racist component.

One can gain a sense of what all this furor was about by looking at the lead article by Gravelli in *Antieuropa* in the winter of 1930. The article is entitled *"Verso l'internazionale fascista"* ("Toward the Fascist International"), and begins with a definition of Gravelli's own group. Typically, that definition placed it in a European context:

> *Antieuropa* is the avant-garde of European fascism. Its task is to group together the best elements in Europe, to instill the experiences of fascism, to nourish the revolutionary fascist spirit, and to establish devotion to the cause of European dictatorship.
> . . . The conquest of power in Italy was only the beginning of a European action. . . .[28]

With the notable exception of the new emphasis on dictatorship, we have heard this language elsewhere, specifically in the journals of young Italians calling for the renovation of their own country. And in keeping with Mussolini's desire to involve youth in the expansion of fascism, Gravelli defined the project of spreading the fascist gospel beyond the boundaries of Italy as one which awaited the genius of fascist youth: "This is why we are anticipating and preparing the union of the young forces of the West. Our modern idea in Europe is a *becoming*, as opposed to a *being* incapable of progress."[29]

Just as the spokesmen for Italian youth had attempted to define their role as that of participants in a generational struggle, the notion of universal fascism came to be cast in battlefield analogies by its proponents. This was, of course, in keeping with fascism's origins in the trenches of World War I, with its early ties to D'Annunzio, and with its reiterated belief in the moral virtues which emerged from struggle. This theme was voiced in the usual melodramatic tones of the Duce in his message for the year IX of the Fascist Era (1931–32):

> The struggle between the two worlds does not admit of compromise, the new cycle which begins with the year IX puts the

dramatic alternative in ever-clearer relief. Either them or us.
Our ideas or theirs. Our State or theirs! . . .

This explains why the struggle is now unfolding on a worldwide scale, and how fascism is the order of the day in all countries. . . .[30]

The struggle was one between two conceptions of the world,
and the Italian fascist response to the worldwide crisis was a
message of youth. In 1932, Gravelli made this theme explicit
when he collected many of his articles from the previous two
years and expanded them into a volume with the same title as
his earlier article, *Verso l'internazionale fascista.* Imitating
Mussolini's syntax, Gravelli set down the conflict in clear terms:
"Either old Europe or young Europe. We hold to a new pact
of European fraternity and discard the old ideas. . . . Fascism
is the gravedigger of old Europe. Now the forces of the Fascist
International are rising."[31]

The similarity between this kind of appeal and that of groups
like the one around *L'Universale* hardly needs to be labored.
What is significant for us is that Gravelli, unlike Berto Ricci,
can be considered an authoritative spokesman for the Fascist
Regime, and that what had been a fascist heresy in certain
quarters had now become official policy. It will be recalled that
the contributors to many of the youth journals put great
emphasis upon the development of genuine creativity, a creativity which would demonstrate the viability of fascism as a
liberator of human genius. Similarly, the kind of association
which Gravelli and his followers conceived as a "Fascist International" would insist upon the development of national fascisms
which were not necessarily to be carbon copies of the Italian
Fascist State. Because "the Europe of tomorrow will be
dominated by Youth," it was not possible for spokesmen of the
present order to lay down firm guidelines for fascism's future
development. Furthermore the very nature of this future devel-

opment in countries other than Italy made any prediction dubious. Fascism would undoubtedly take a variety of forms; and the specific form of collaboration between these different fascist revolutions could not be anticipated.

The program of Gravelli and his followers was therefore designed to ensure the maximum flexibility for each national fascism, provided only that it meet certain "spiritual" criteria. This concept is best illustrated through Gravelli's definition of a fascist dictatorship, found in a special number of *Antieuropa* given over entirely to this question in 1933.[32] Gravelli's interesting conception of the fascist dictatorship is that the figure of the dictator himself logically and historically precedes the institution of the dictatorship. The figure of the national dictator emerges from the nation's struggle for survival, whereas in other forms of revolution (as, for example, the Communist Revolution) the movement itself is committed in advance to the establishment of a dictatorship. True dictators, says Gravelli, emerge only in periods of great crisis and political chaos. Consequently such genuine leaders as Napoleon, Hitler, Mussolini, and Mustafa Kemal could never have been the products of a merely political coup and change in institutions; the dynamism of their rule stemmed from the dialectic of the process which brought them to power.

This brings us back to the notion of the new "fascist man" dealt with at the end of the preceding chapter. Given the vagueness of fascist doctrine, or, perhaps more accurately, the many different fascist doctrines current at the time, the focus of the call for a fascist awakening in Europe centered less on institutional change than on a spiritual transformation of Europeans. The point was driven home by Gravelli many times, perhaps most clearly on June 5, 1934, in *Ottobre*:

> . . . It is not enough to change the institutions. We have stated and repeated this a hundred times: the men and their mentality

must be changed. In other words, revolutions are great spiritual facts, before being economic, social, and political facts.

It appears that all this has not been considered carefully enough in certain foreign areas, where it is believed with a certain aplomb that one can imitate or duplicate fascism.[33]

Gravelli's message was designed to appeal to many who had grown somewhat disgruntled with fascism, and also served a useful function for Mussolini. Yet the subsequent development of the *Antieuropa* movement leaves little doubt that it ultimately became something of an embarrassment to the regime, and that Gravelli and his followers may have become too enthusiastic in their pursuit of a Fascist International.

The concrete stimulus for the expansion of Gravelli's group came in reaction to one of Mussolini's showpieces in honor of the first decade of fascism, the Volta Congress. As part of the celebration of fascism's first decade in power, Mussolini organized a vast international Congress on Europe, named in honor of the noted Italian scientist Alessandro Volta. Held under the auspices of the Italian Academy, the Volta Congress met in Rome in November, 1932, to listen to the prognostications and ideas of some of the most distinguished European intellectuals favorable to the fascist regime. The list of dignitaries constituted a representative cross section of European rightist thought in the early thirties, ranging from the most outspoken Nazis to those sympathetic to anti-racist, Corporatist conceptions of society. Delegates included Daniel Halévy and Pierre Gaxotte from France; Werner Sombart, Alfred Rosenberg, Hjalmar Schacht, and Hermann Goering from Germany; Prince Rohan and Stefan Zweig from Austria; Mihail Manoilesco from Rumania, and other noted conservative and reactionary figures from the continent. The two major powers without representation at the Congress were Great Britain and the Soviet Union.[34]

The discussions were undoubtedly gratifying to the organi-

zers, since for the most part the speakers hurled elaborate verbal
bouquets at the feet of the Duce. The theme of the Congress,
"On Europe," produced a number of reflections on the twentieth-century crisis, as well as a kind of spiritual geopolitics which
saw Europe menaced by a Soviet-led Africa and Asia on the
one hand, and by America and England on the other. The thrust
of many of the speeches was for the spiritual revivification of
Europe, and most of them looked towards fascist Italy for the
inspiration needed. To be sure, National Socialists and other
nonfascists were at the Congress and spoke their piece; but the
clear sentiment of the delegates was for Roman leadership and
Italian fascist guidance. The major concern of the delegates was
fear of a Communist Revolution, and Mussolini was repeatedly
hailed as having been the first great leader in Europe to have
effectively routed the Bolshevik menace in his own country,
thus serving as an example for the rest of the world.[35]

This celebration of Italian achievements could not help but
inspire those who had been agitating for a Fascist International,
and predictably Gravelli wrote about the Congress in glowing
terms. His report appeared on January 15, 1933, in *Ottobre*.
After an account of the events of the Congress, Gravelli called
for a meeting of "Young Europe," of the forces for that revivification the delegates to the Congress had demanded but were
unable to provide:

> . . . Prepared in men's spirits, realized by the situation, vital to
> the life of the future, this Young Europe has already carried its
> crown of flowers to the tombs of the crushed ideals of the
> entire Old World . . . [men feel] that in Rome, and in fascism,
> vibrates all the poetry of an original world. . . .[36]

The Volta Congress had indicated that the terrain had been
prepared for a movement of European youth. The remarkable
support for Mussolini which the older representatives of continental culture and politics had demonstrated was simply a

fraction of the enthusiasm for fascism which lay untapped beneath the surface of European ferment. This judgment was evidently quite widespread among fascist leaders, for less than a week later the Rome correspondent of *Le Temps* reported on conversations he had heard in "fascist circles":

> It is said that the Volta Congress . . . only brought together the representatives of the old generation, attached by a thousand ties to the liberal and democratic ideal. Now it is time to convoke, on the banks of the Tiber, the representatives of European youth desirous of a profound reform in the spirit of our continent, based on the ideas of order and authority.[37]

The cry launched early in 1933 was for an organization of the spirit of Youth, and the Italians were quick to seize upon this slogan, tied as it was to their own revolutionary history. Recalling that nearly a century before Mazzini had organized the movement of Young Italy, the writers for *Ottobre* called for a movement to be called "Young Europe," to be touched off by a Youth Congress.[38]

This cry for the organization of the forces of Youth all over Europe met with considerable support outside Italy. In addition to the declaration of support from Paris, Gravelli received letters from Colonel Fonjallez, the leader of Swiss fascism, and Simon Ooms, the head of a group of Dutch fascists.[39] It is significant that at no point in the discussions on Young Europe (which lasted well over a year) was Nazi participation strongly supported, nor did any initiative come from the German National Socialists. From the very beginning of the agitation for an international organization of fascisms, contributors to *Ottobre* warned of the dangers of association with the Nazis. Typical of this attitude is the warning delivered by a Dutch fascist named Jan Baars in December, 1933, who deplored Nazi antisemitism (a position supported by Gravelli), and warned that Hitler sought a homogeneous state, and the expansion of German suzerainty over a gigantic *Deutschtum*.[40]

In any event, by July *Ottobre* could begin to spell out the kind of structure the proposed international movement would have. It is worth looking at this proposal at some length:

> . . . It must be stressed that the International—precisely because it will be baptized by an élite of free and unprejudiced men, not tied in any way to any government, not even to one of the Fascist States—will assume with full consciousness responsibility for the action . . . it proposes to launch and will launch in the world.
>
> The full and absolute independence of the International and of its sections from all governments must be solemnly affirmed and guaranteed.
>
> At the same time the Fascist International, which will gather to its bosom men who put their love for their own countries at the base of their internationalism, must take an oath never to impede the work of states and of responsible governments aimed at international collaboration. . . .
>
> We conceive of the Fascist International according to the teachings of Mazzini: "Like a militant church with a task to achieve."[41]

As the weeks passed, the proponents of the new International developed ever more elaborate schemes. They began to distinguish between élitist and mass elements, and by the summer of 1933 bitter debates over the possible inclusion of German Nazis and their sympathizers had broken out in the pages of both *Ottobre* and *Antieuropa*.[42]

It would be a serious mistake, however, to limit our analysis to these journals. A veritable outburst of journals, newspapers, *ad hoc* groups, and the like was busy attempting to organize some sort of international body for the expansion of fascism. To get some notion of the phenomenon involved here we shall consider two such groups.

The year 1932 saw the first appearance of a bi-monthly journal entitled *Universalità Romana* (*Roman Universality*), under the direction of a distinguished economist from Milan, Carlo Emilio Ferri. In addition to his journalistic activities, Ferri

was associated with two organizations in Milan that were tied
in various ways to the attempt to found a Fascist International.
These were the *Circolo Filologico Milanese* (The Milan Philo-
logical Circle) and the *Centro di Studi Internazionale sul fascismo* (Center of International Studies of Fascism).

The *Circolo Filologico Milanese* was a fascinating group,
ostensibly dedicated to the development of Italian culture. In
practice, it seems to have been a kind of international clearing-
house for men and ideas sympathetic to the cause of international fascism. Virtually every important foreign fascist leader
who passed through Milan in the early thirties gave an address
at the *Circolo*, and many of those in Italy involved in the
attempt to found an International appeared there as well.
Gravelli himself spoke at the *Circolo* in February, 1933.[43]
When the Swiss fascist leader Georges Oltramare came to Milan
in May, 1933, he spoke there, as did Goebbels the following
month.[44] As director of this organization, Ferri was in the
forefront of contacts with non-Italian fascists; his semi-official
status as a representative of the Italian cultural community lends
his writing considerable importance.

The *Centro di Studi Internazionale sul fascismo* was one of
a great many such institutes formally designed to encourage the
study of fascism, but actually centers for the distribution of
fascist propaganda. Organizations of this sort appeared at a
remarkable rate in the early thirties, and one of the most famous
was the CINEF, the *Centre International d'Études sur le Fascisme*, located in Lausanne, Switzerland, under the leadership
of an Englishman, James Strachey Barnes. A brief digression is
in order here if we are to understand the nature of these
institutes, which constituted a principal means of circulating
fascist propaganda in the thirties.

The primary source of information about the operation of the
Lausanne Center comes from its 1928 *Yearbook*,[45] the only
year in which the publication appeared. The Center had a

genuinely international governing body, headed by Barnes himself as secretary general, and a three-man executive council, composed of H. De Vries De Heekelingen (formerly a professor at the University of Nijmegen), Marcel Boulenger, and Giovanni Gentile. The other members of the governing body were A. Andreades, professor at the University of Athens; Antonio Aunós, director of publications of the Joint Commission of Employers and Employees of Catalonia; Count Thadee Dzieduszyckie of Warsaw; Istvan Ereky, professor at the University of Szeged, Hungary; C. Fougner of Oslo; Edmund Gardner, F.B.A., professor at the University of London; A. Geouffre de Lapradelle, professor at the University of Paris; John L. Gerig, professor at Columbia University; Jonkheer J. W. Godin De Beaufort of Holland; Nae Ionescu, professor at the University of Bucharest; Ladislas Jablonowski, member of the Polish Senate; J. W. Mannhardt, professor at the University of Marburg; J. Renkin, Minister of State in Brussels; Baron Rolin Jaequemyns, formerly Belgian Minister of the Interior; Walter Starkie, professor at Trinity College, Dublin; Lord Sydenham of Combe, London; Count Paul Teleki, former Hungarian Minister of Foreign Affairs; and M. W. F. Treub, formerly Dutch Minister of Finance.[46]

This not undistinguished assemblage of intellectuals had undertaken to spread the fascist message to the world outside Italy. The work of missionary devotion was masked by the formal declaration of purpose which De Heekelingen announced in the 1928 *Yearbook*:

> The "Cinef" intends to abstain from the expression of any opinion of its own on Fascism. It proposes . . . to furnish the means by which the student may be enabled to lay his hands on anything of importance that has been published on the subject. . . .[47]

Yet a brief survey of the *Yearbook*'s contents is sufficient to remove any doubts as to the true nature of the Center. The articles included "The Birth and Establishment of Fascism in Italy" by Gioacchino Volpe, the "official" historian of the Italian Fascist Regime; "The Civil Strife in Italy, 1919–1922," a violently anti-socialist polemic by Luigi Villari; "The Significance of Fascist Syndicalism" by the apostle of the Fascist Syndicalist movement in Italy, Edmundo Rossoni; "The Labor Charter" by the Secretary of the Fascist Party, Augusto Turati; and "The Reform of the State in Italy" by Barnes, who had recently published a book of his own on the universality of fascism. It is therefore clear that the Center was at the very least supported by the intellectual output of some of the most important members of the Italian fascist hierarchy. This sympathy was further demonstrated by the fact that Mussolini contributed an Introduction to Barnes' book, *The Universal Aspects of Fascism.*[48]

The *Yearbook*, in article after article, stressed the uniqueness of Italian fascism in offering guidelines to other societies for solving their common problems, and also tried to show the benevolence of Italy toward other versions of fascism. "One of the main postulates of fascism," De Heekelingen told his readers, "is indeed that there can exist no particular form of government capable of serving as a model at all times and places."[49] Thus, even though the particular institutions which the Italian fascists had developed in the peninsula might not appeal to potential fascists in other countries, the inspiration for these institutions might find another expression abroad.

This theme was developed at great length by Barnes in *The Universal Aspects of Fascism*, a ponderous work which invoked the intellectual support of figures ranging from St. Thomas Aquinas to Alfred North Whitehead in behalf of fascist "doctrine." In attempting to demonstrate that many of Italian fascism's institutions need not be considered essential to fascism itself, Barnes took the evolution of Mussolini's dictatorship as a paradigm. "Fascism does not stand for a dictatorship, neither of a person nor of a class. . . . If there is a dictatorship in Italy now, it is because the revolutionary organisation has taken this form by an accident of history."[50] The same could be said of the Corporate State:

> Mussolini rightly considers that the best form of Government is the one which, in the given circumstances of a particular country, works best. So Fascism does not and cannot absolutely condemn popular Government, for instance. . . . Nor does Fascism, conversely, stand absolutely by the idea of the "Corporative State." . . . These matters are contingent. . . .[51]

Barnes' notion of fascism, in short, was one of a successful movement which might inspire other governments to abandon the outmoded principles of Western civilization: *laissez-faire* economics, liberalism, and above all socialism and communism. His goal for the future was, interestingly enough, that of the end of all nations, the unification of mankind under a single structure. However, he argued that national fascism was the most appropriate route toward this destiny:

> Fascism insists that progress towards this goal can only be made by upholding the principle of authority in existing States, and not, as would humanitarian Internationalists, by weakening authority and national sentiment, which sustains authority. . . .[52]

Thus the adherents to universal fascism would not be asked to sacrifice any of their national integrity, but simply to join in the common search for the true expression of national genius wherever the forces of the modern world expressed themselves. As such, fascism was clearly a harbinger of things to come, and Barnes set it firmly against the system of the past by stating that "the present *Weltanschauung* of Fascism may be summed up in one word: *Youth*."[53]

In his development of the ideal of fascist Youth, Barnes explicitly voiced a sentiment which in Italian debates had often remained slightly beneath the surface: the inability of the generation in power to achieve a truly fascist Revolution. Barnes' complaints about the "middle generation" sound strikingly like those of many of the youthful intellectuals we have discussed earlier, and show again the close relationship between universal fascism and the cult of Youth:

> . . . the men between 30 and 45, represent a more difficult proposition; and I doubt if they can, as a whole, be transformed into the complete Fascist.
> The speeches of Mussolini and of . . . Turati have only to be read and it will be realized how hard the leaders of Fascism hammer the rank and file, who will not or cannot live the Fascist ideal. But the process is undoubtedly telling and the result is a new generation growing up, who promise to make a governing class really worthy of the ideal. . . .[54]

In short, the Fascist Revolution was a revolution of man, and could be said to have succeeded when and only when men's ideas and behavior had been drastically changed.

Barnes also devoted much attention to the Christian component of fascism, repeatedly claiming that the "true" philosopher of fascism was St. Thomas Aquinas.[55] This stress upon the religious element in the Roman synthesis would receive considerable attention from many of the advocates of universal fascism, among them Carlo Emilio Ferri and the group around *Universalità Romana*.

As a testimony to the cosmopolitan nature of its readership, *Universalità Romana* carried articles in many different languages. Ferri was devoted to Arnaldo Mussolini, and the first issue of his journal carried a long article by Arnaldo on the universal implications of fascism. Further, the motto of the journal reinforced Arnaldo's emphasis on the religious nature of fascism: "Religion and fascism are the key to life." This emphasis on the religious component of fascism was common to many, but by no means all, of the propagandists for universal fascism.

Ferri's personal vision was presented to the readers of *Universalità Romana* in its second issue, in an article (written in French) entitled *Pour une Union Intellectuelle Fasciste* ("For an Intellectual Fascist Union"). His analysis of the crisis of the West and the prospects for its cure ran along "standard" lines: ". . . Everyone agrees with the proposition that Europe and the entire world can only find health in an idea, the creative force of which can give new youth to the West. . . ."[56]

Yet when Ferri turned to his proposal for the organization of a union, he restricted it to intellectuals, and went out of his way to state that he was not, at least for the time being, interested in attempting to organize a full-scale International. Noting that "many among us have advanced the more ambitious project of wanting to constitute a veritable Fascist International," Ferri maintained that such an ambitious enterprise was premature, feeling that the immediate appeal of fascism was not yet sufficiently powerful to permit the realization of a viable political organization on an international scale. He was nonetheless convinced that fascism had achieved tremendous popularity and penetration among two crucial groups in the West: the intellectuals and the young. To these two elements, Ferri added a third: surprisingly enough, "workers' organizations." This was tied to the usual polemic eulogizing the fascist achievement of "social justice," and, not surprisingly, working-class organizations were not mentioned again in Ferri's program. Instead, his focus was upon European youth:

> It is youth which has a distaste for traditional political doctrines, for parliamentary dreams, for the vague and hypocritical words of internationalism: everywhere youth considers the "Nation" to be the central kernel of the new order. . . .
> The future lies with youth. It is to the youth of "Young Europe" that a fascist Intellectual Union must address itself. . . .[57]

This clearly put Ferri in harmony with the general aims of the *Antieuropa* group, and the similarity in their rhetoric turns out to have been more than fortuitous. Ferri and Gravelli had been in contact with each other,[58] and obviously directed their activities so as to compliment one another. Both traveled widely, in Italy and Europe, and attempted to generate continental enthusiasm for their programs. Working through various centers of propaganda, including the School of Fascist Mysticism in Milan, Ferri managed to attract an international editorial board for *Universalità Romana*.[59] And, like Gravelli, he solicited and received a large volume of support and encouragement from various foreign fascist groups, all anxious to participate in the coming International, whatever form it might eventually take.

In this process of attempting to organize propaganda centers, many organizations already in existence before the campaign for universal fascism were able to change their direction and join the great adventure. One such was associated with Ferri's group, the *Istututo di studi romani*. This had been founded in 1925, and had been headed by such notable figures as Professor Pietro Fedele and Luigi Federzoni, the former Nationalist leader. Mussolini himself was honorary president of the Institute, which had been dedicated to the furtherance of Latin, or "Roman" culture. By the winter of 1932 it was clearly involved in the activities of Ferri and his colleagues. Its goal was that of winning converts to the Roman revelation:

> . . . Its aim is . . . to create in Italy, and especially abroad, cultural centers of Roman studies on a vast scale, which will recultivate on the ruins of the anti-Romanic world . . . the great Western culture which can no longer live without Rome as its center and guide.[60]

Groups of this sort, aimed at various kinds of audiences abroad, became widespread during the middle thirties. Ruggero Zangrandi has testified to the ease with which they were organized, and the wide range of organizations willing to sponsor them.[61] Whether under the direction of the GUF, the Party itself, or the Ministry of Popular Culture, people who were trusted by the regime and who were recognized in the field of journalism and propaganda were invariably given the opportunity to participate in this movement to create a Fascist International. As might be expected, centers appeared and disappeared with great regularity, depending upon their state of favor in Rome. Whatever the particular title, they were often in fact simply sinecures for the friends of fascist hierarchs, the profits of the fascist spoils system.

Yet having said this, it must still be recognized that there were serious elements at work within this network of men and organizations. We will see in the next chapter that Mussolini for a time tried to channel this activity through a single organization and that a considerable amount of money and energy was spent trying to support this attempt to organize an International under official auspices. But at this stage it is necessary to stress two things. First, it seems clear that the notion of the potential application of fascist doctrine to problems outside the Italian peninsula was a viable one for many Italians and for foreigners as well. Second, the cult of youth played an essential role in this concept of expansion, and many young Italian intellectuals were anxious to fulfill the doctrinal prophecies.

This close connection between youth and universal fascism is demonstrated in yet another group engaged in the formulation of fascist ideology, that formed around Oddone Fantini and Carlo Curcio and their journal, *Universalità Fascista* (*Fascist University*). Fantini and Curcio were two highly respected and rather distinguished older intellectuals. Fantini, born in 1890, had won a gold medal for valor in the Great War, held a chair of Political Economy and Finance at the University of Rome, and had become the director of the Fascist Institute of Culture there. Curcio, a Neapolitan, was born in 1898 and was Professor of the History of Political Doctrine at the University of Perugia. Fantini had founded a journal in 1929 called *Università Fascista* (*The Fascist University*), a monthly review of university activities in Italy. Two years later, in May, 1931, he changed its title and scope, and it became "a monthly review of revolutionary expansion and Italian university life."

Well aware of the existence of other journals dealing with the "revolutionary expansion" of fascism, the editors of *Universalità Fascista* were careful to distinguish between their own goals and those of others, pointing out that while *Universalità Romana*, for example, was dedicated to spreading the message of universal fascism, the goal of *Universalità Fascista* was to be the clarification and study of fascist doctrine.[62] Their efforts over the next two years were summarized by Fantini in a volume published in 1933 entitled *Universalità del Fascismo* (*Universality of Fascism*). The introduction by Curcio anticipated Fantini's analysis:

> Nothing, ever, in the history of a people is as powerful as the idea . . . [the fascist idea] is above all a *moral* idea: a new ethic in the relationships of the society, a new faith in men themselves and in the Nation, and a new character, a new civil religion.[63]

The stress on morals is very close to the call for the new "fascist man" encountered elsewhere, and Fantini elaborated on this fundamental theme at great length. As one would expect from a man who had directed a journal dedicated to universities, he stressed the role of education in creating the new fascist generation. Noting that various fascist organizations were involved in the education of youth from an early age, Fantini expressed his confidence that the new generation would provide a solid guarantee of the durability of fascism: "In this way fascism has provided for the creation of new human material, the new people, that is to say, the indispensable precondition for making the new political and economic order a lasting one. . . ."[64]

For Fantini and Curcio, then, fascism meant more than simply the establishment of a set of institutions, or spreading the institutions of Fascist Italy to other countries. The Corporate State, for example, important though it might have been, was not the same thing as the Fascist State. Further, just as Mussolini had not come to power with a specific program, it would be preposterous to demand that other fascist leaders copy the doctrines of the Duce, especially since that program was not a rigid one, but in the process of development.

The spokesmen for the creation of a Fascist International were insistent on this point: that the expansion of fascism guaranteed considerable integrity and initiative to non-Italian fascisms. This represented an extension of the principle (outlined earlier) that the creation of a durable fascism in Italy awaited the creativity and energy of a new generation. If fascism in Italy was "incomplete," then it would be preposterous to export an imperfect product. Yet the impetus for a new society and a new man *was* present in Italy, and this drive for the creation of a new order was something which could be extended beyond Italian boundaries.

The notion of universal fascism as a new doctrine for a new world thus infused the movement for the creation of a Fascist International, and the International increasingly came to be viewed as a way of focusing discontent with existing institutions, both in Italy and in Europe as a whole. The appeal which this notion held for young fascist intellectuals should be clear. Not only would Italy be revivified, but this transformation would extend throughout the world.

It must be stressed again, however, that despite the internationalist rhetoric, Italian problems and Italian society remained

at the center of the debates surrounding the creation of the
International. Indeed, one frequently finds articles reminding
adherents of the International that their first task was the creation of a viable Italian fascism, and above all the elucidation of a
coherent fascist doctrine within the Italian tradition. Without
the Italian paradigm, the creation of a Fascist International
would be mere fantasy.

In the edition of *Fascismo Universale* he published in 1933,
for example, Gastone Silvano Spinetti used the call for a Fascist
International as the basis to return to one of his basic themes:
the need to construct a coherent and dynamic fascist doctrine
capable of demonstrating the vitality of the movement. He
argued that before a successful international organization could
be created, it would be necessary for numerous national conferences to be held in order to fully elaborate fascist doctrine.

> In such conventions . . . it will be necessary to demonstrate how
> fascism, even though it is the expression of the civilization of the
> new times, is not opposed to tradition and culture, and how such
> culture is not that Celtic one from beyond our frontiers, because
> [that foreign culture] is atheist, individualist, and anti-national.[65]

The reference to "Celtic" German National Socialism, while
somewhat oblique, remained a major theme in the writings of
the proponents of universal fascism and was to play a major role
in the debates concerning a Fascist International. But Spinetti's
insistence on clarifying Italian fascist doctrine is clearly a thinly
veiled critique of Italian fascism itself, and provided him with
the opportunity to call once again for a systematic formulation
of fascist theory. He was not alone in this desire.

The very vagueness of official fascist theory, especially as to
the practical possibilities of exporting fascism, gave the advocates of universal fascism the opportunity to attempt all kinds of
initiatives, ranging from the efforts of such people as Oddone
Fantini and Carlo Emilio Ferri to organize groups of European

intellectuals in propaganda centers, to those of Asvero Gravelli to hold a conference on "Young Europe." All of this activity was of course duly noted by Mussolini and could not but have produced some anxiety in Palazzo Venezia. The kind of spontaneity frequently associated with these groups and, more importantly, the kind of criticism of the regime (although not, of course, of Mussolini himself) implicit in the demand for universal fascism, combined to suggest to many around the dictator that the organizations might be masks for some genuinely anti-fascist activity. As a result, surveillance over these groups was increased, and by 1935, if not earlier, OVRA and other secret police elements were watching the participants regularly.[66] If some of their activities became excessive, the groups were generally warned by one of the hierarchs, and if the behavior was not terminated, the groups were simply dissolved.

The program of "exporting" fascism beyond Italy did not suffer from any lack of organizations devoted to such activity.[67] We have already seen that there were various *ad hoc* centers for the dissemination of fascist propaganda abroad, and mention must be made of three other official organizations, in order to give a more complete picture of the range of these bodies: the *Fasci all'estero* (Fascist Groups Abroad), the *Società Dante Alighieri* (Dante Alighieri Society), and the *Scuola di Mistica Fascista* (School of Fascist Mysticism). The last was discussed earlier in another connection, but its activities in generating propaganda must be dealt with here as well.

The *Fasci all'estero* were the official organizations for all Italians living outside the boundaries of the peninsula, and included activities which parallelled those provided at home for native Italians.[68] Thus, young Italians living abroad could participate in the *Balilla*, and so forth. The Dante Alighieri Society was a worldwide organization for the study of Italian culture, and during the fascist *Ventennio* provided a useful means of coordinating the propaganda activities of numerous groups of fascists living abroad.[69] The School of Fascist Mysticism was one of the major centers for the editing, publication, and distribution of books dealing with the fascist message. In 1933, *Universalità Romana* carried an advertisement for various books published by the School, and some of the titles show the extent to which Arnaldo's School for the creation of a new élite had become involved in the spread of the doctrines of universal fascism. They included Arnaldo's own *Coscienza e dovere* (*Conscience and Duty*), *L'eredità spirituale di Giuseppe Mazzini* (*The Spiritual Heritage of Mazzini*) by Gianni Poletti, and *Orizzonti imperiali* (*Imperial Horizons*) by Valentino Piccoli.[70] Bearing in mind the other organizations mentioned earlier, the number of groups acting on behalf of the prestige of the fascist regime was quite impressive. But the problem of groups agitating for a "spontaneous" Fascist International, outside the framework of any government, remained unsolved.

That segment of the press dealing with universal fascism found itself able to say things which would undoubtedly have been censored coming from other areas. The most likely explanation for this is that fascist foreign policy during the early and middle thirties was in a constant state of flux, and consequently proposals for the creation of a Fascist International were not immediately evaluated in the context of a coherent foreign strategy. Not only was the question of Italy's relation to the League of Nations under careful review, but the emergence of Nazi Germany posed a whole series of problems for the Foreign Office. We shall deal with this in greater detail later on, but for now it must be said that Mussolini's original response to Hitler was overwhelmingly negative. Yet Mussolini was to be personally intrigued by the *Führer*, and the existence of initial secret contacts between the two dictators suggests that the full story of the early relations between Hitler and Mussolini remains to be written.

From the standpoint of universal fascism, the existence of Nazi Germany simply involved a special case of a more general problem, which might be termed the problem of foreign fascisms. In the early and middle thirties all manner of political movements emerged calling themselves "fascist," and more often than not such movements proclaimed their fealty to Mussolini and to Italian fascism. What was the regime to do about these foreign groups? One thing was becoming increasingly clear: if the government failed to institutionalize the activities directed towards the formation of a Fascist International, it might very well find such an organization established outside official fascist structures. This was clearly intolerable to Mussolini, and he moved quickly to co-opt the movement for a Fascist International.

It might be thought that the problem of foreign fascisms was a relatively simple one, given that a small number of fascist movements emerged before the actual outbreak of the Second World War. Such, however, is not the case, for there was an incredible proliferation of fascist movements across the European continent in the interwar period. Unless one has looked at some of the literature surrounding the proposed Fascist International, it is hard to imagine just how many fascist groups apparently existed in the middle thirties. Literally dozens of them appeared briefly, then vanished back into the chaotic background of European politics. Yet each one posed a serious dilemma for the regime, and for the would-be organizers of an International of fascisms. In each case it was necessary to decide whether the group in question was genuinely fascist, and whether it was worth the time, energy, and (often) money to encourage their activities. In fact, the Italian government spent a great deal of money financing foreign fascist movements in the thirties. The two best-known cases are of course the Austrian *Heimwehr* and the Belgian Rexists,[71] but considerable sums were distributed somewhat indirectly as well. Given a tight fiscal situation in Italy, the regime wanted to make sure it got a decent return on its investment.

As a consequence of these problems, many of the journals dealing with the expansion of fascism undertook to analyze these foreign movements case by case, in an attempt to ascertain which of them were worthy of inclusion in a Fascist International. At times the question was very difficult, since the journalists might decide that a movement claiming to be fascist was phony, while some of the hierarchs in Rome felt otherwise. An even more perplexing problem involved the Spanish Falange, which claimed *not* to be fascist, but looked for all the world like a paradigm of a foreign fascism.[72] In a lengthy analysis for *Universalità Fascista* in 1936, Spinetti argued that the Falange was a true fascist movement because of its belief in the fascist trinity of "authority, hierarchy, order," and because of the Spanish "mysticism" which raised Falangist principles to a universal plane.[73]

Other fascist movements were subjected to careful scrutiny by the writers of *Ottobre*. The Irish Blue Shirts, under the leadership of Colonel O'Duffy, were considered a true fascist movement,[74] and Salazar's Portugal gained the stamp of approval early in 1933.[75] A figure like Vidkun Quisling, however, received ambivalent treatment from the advocates of universal fascism, who admired his qualities as "a man of action," but had some serious reservations about his racist ideas.[76] Various Dutch parties came under scrutiny, and *Ottobre* supported such figures as J. C. Baars and Ooms,[77] but considered Mussert unworthy of the fascist label.[78] The Austrian *Heimwehr* were hailed enthusiastically,[79] and when Starhemberg came to Rome in April, 1934, he granted an extended interview to *Ottobre* in which he proclaimed his support for Mussolini and his antagonism to National Socialist principles.[80] In France, *Ottobre* saw only one true fascist movement, the *Jeunesses Patriotes*;[81] the *Action Française* was considered too traditional, and Marcel Bucard's *Franciste* movement was rejected because of the federalist doctrines of its leader.[82]

While there was considerable debate over various movements claiming to be fascist, there was very little argument over the nature of German National Socialism. From the very beginning the Nazis were branded heretics of the first order, and throughout the period under consideration here the press continued to attack the "pagan" racism of the Nazis.[83] Mussolini himself was unsparing in his denunciations of Nazi racial theory, once calling *Mein Kampf* "that incoherent tirade I have never managed to read,"[84] and terming Hitler's doctrine 10 per cent science and 90 per cent sentiment.[85] Further, from the point of view of the advocates of a fascist organization on an international scale, the German brand of military expansion and the Nazi concept of a *Reich*, which was little more than an expansion of Germany's borders, were anathema.

The theme of anti-Nazism became ever more pronounced with the success of Hitler's regime, as the Italian propagandists saw that the predominance of Mussolini on the European scene was being considerably weakened by the *Führer*. In fact, if there is a single theme which dominates the literature of the period, it is the tension between Rome and Berlin, the antagonism between fascism and Nazism. This is brought out well in a special issue of *Antieuropa* in the winter of 1933,[86] entirely given over to the question of racism. Fascist after fascist wrote of the folly of the racist doctrine, stressed the humanistic and religious components of Italian fascism, and attacked Hitler.

As if to symbolize the antagonism to the Nazis, the special number of *Antieuropa* began with an excerpt from Mussolini's introduction to the Italian edition of Richard Korherr's *Regression of the Birth Rate, Death of Peoples*, which put forth the theory that a concentration of populations in cities produced a drop in a people's potency. Mussolini summed it up nicely, with particular emphasis on the most afflicted spot on the globe:

> The progressive sterility of citizens is in direct relation to the monstrous rapid growth of the city. Berlin, which in a single century has passed from 100,000 to over 4,000,000 inhabitants, is today the most sterile city in the world.[87]

This slur on the vitality of the German capital was only the beginning of an extended assault on Nazi doctrines. The final denunciation came from Gravelli, after a lengthy analysis of the nature of Nazi racism and an exploration of its political consequences. "We are," he told his readers, "the protestants of the racist religion; we refute this faith and believe in the reality of facts, not in a presumed reality which does not correspond to the truth."[88]

All these conflicts necessitated some action by Mussolini, since proclamations of adherence to the International on the one hand and philo-Nazi cries of anger on the other were flooding into the offices of the various journalistic headquarters. Mussolini's response was to attempt to bring the entire movement under control as best he could. Where possible, he simply brought some of the independent groups under the auspices of an already existing official organization, such as the GUF.[89] But that still left a large sphere of activity untouched. To bring these other groups under his control, Mussolini organized the *Comitati d'azione per l'Universalità di Roma* (the Action Committees for Roman Universality, known as the CAUR), under the direction of Eugenio Coselschi, a veteran of the Great War, and formerly D'Annunzio's private secretary in Fiume in 1920. At the banquet celebrating the foundation of the CAUR in

June, 1933, Coselschi paid tribute to Gravelli and his allies for having generated much support for the creation of an international organization for the universality of fascism, but the tone of his speech was such as to create considerable apprehension among the staff of *Ottobre*, who rightly saw the CAUR as a menace to their own continued activities.

Despite the anxieties of those who had been in the forefront of the struggle to create an International, it nonetheless seemed that their long journalistic campaign had been crowned by success. Although the formal organization of the International might be in the hands of a relative newcomer to the battlefield, the war itself seemed about to be waged. We must now turn to the international sphere in order to consider the activities of the CAUR, and to examine the outcome of this romantic attempt to fulfill a Mazzinian vision under the rubric of universal fascism.

CHAPTER FOUR

The Fascist International

.∧∧.∧ The emergence of the *Comitati d'azione per l'Universalità di Roma* must be viewed as a significant act by Mussolini, who thereby confirmed institutionally that his famous claim: "Fascism is not merchandise for export" had been proven wrong by the course of events. There was, indeed, a considerable market abroad for fascist output. Shaken to its foundations by the worldwide economic depression of the early thirties, torn over demands for revision of the Versailles Treaties, distressed and perplexed by the emergence of Hitler's Nazi State from the ruins of Weimar, "old Europe" appeared to be on the verge of complete transformation. For many of the alarmed statesmen and intellectuals in centers of power, Mussolini's Italy seemed to offer the possibility of a new model for Western nations, and Roosevelt's request for a study of the Italian Corporate State is symptomatic of this state of mind in 1933. In the whirlpool of Western society, many seemed willing to grasp at the apparently buoyant straw of fascism.

As the eyes of the world turned toward Rome in search of solutions to their increasingly urgent problems, Mussolini himself apparently came to believe in the universal destiny of fascism.[1] The centers for fascist propaganda were created partly in response to genuine interest abroad, and partly because Mussolini was desperately searching for enhanced prestige, both at home and abroad. The confirmation of the rightness of his own course of action would mean a universal acclamation for, and adoption of, "fascist" institutions throughout the world. Winning adherents to fascist principles thus became one of the goals of fascist activity, and the object of much of this activity was now European youth.

Within Italy, the expansion of fascism was viewed by some as a continuation of the process of "revolutionizing" it which had begun some time before. This theme was the subject of an editorial in *Critica Fascista* in the summer of 1933:

> The motor of spiritual renovation, which we began in the Italian provinces just a decade ago in the name of revolutionary fascism, only now begins to have repercussions and to produce its first consequences in the life of the young peoples of Europe. . . .
>
> . . . Ours was truly a *politics of the new generation* because it was born out of the confrontation with the traditional systems and forces. . . .[2]

Throughout Italy the call for the creation of a Fascist International was repeatedly joined with the call for the creation of a truly revolutionary fascism, inspired by the spirit of Youth. We have seen how Giuseppe Bottai became the spokesman for many of these young fascists, and Bottai's own stress on the close connection between the expansion of fascism and its increasingly revolutionary nature was paradigmatic for much of the "new generation." But in the early thirties, Bottai's prestige among young fascists was severely challenged by the son-in-law of the Duce, Galeazzo Ciano, soon destined to become the Foreign Minister. For the remainder of the fascist epoch in Italy, young fascists looked primarily to Bottai or Ciano for guidance.[3] Since Ciano was above all involved in foreign affairs, those concerned with the spread of the doctrines of universal fascism more often went to him for support and advice, and were generally pleased by his attitude. Ruggero Zangrandi has described a conversation with Ciano in 1937, when Zangrandi was trying to win support for a Center for International Fascism:

> . . . the "new man," the man of the day, was Galeazzo Ciano.
> . . . More responsible voices attributed to him . . . new and "ardent" ideas, a great dynamism, an obvious mania for popularity and the desire to capture for himself the sympathy of young and renovatory currents, that is to say, of those whom he believed ought to represent the "fresh energies" to which the regime had given birth.
>   He was, therefore, our man. . . . Ciano was not the traditional hierarch. . . . Above all, in my case, he liked to stress that there was only a dozen years' difference between us, and that I offered him the chance to re-establish direct contact with youth, something which he said he valued greatly. . . .[4]

This attitude of Ciano's was of signal importance in the development of the *universalfascismo* movement, for in 1935 Ciano became Undersecretary of Press and Propaganda, and the expansion of the activities of those sections of the press devoted to spreading the message of universal fascism was directly linked to the parallel growth of Ciano's power within the regime.[5]

The desires of Gravelli and Coselschi fitted well with those of the new man within the Fascist Regime, for Ciano was full of ambition and possessed an ego second only to Mussolini's in its need for affection and adulation.[6] Consequently, the tasks of spreading fascist propaganda abroad and gathering tributes to Mussolini and the Fascist State were very congenial to Ciano's talents and personality. And his conception of the role of press and propaganda was calculated to excite the advocates of a Fascist International:

> Shortly, an organization will arise here which will be the first in Italy. Everything will pass through my hands, we will speak to the whole world. We will tell all other countries about Italy

and her great men. We will use radio, theater, and the movies. And, naturally, we will use the press. But above all we will use men.[7]

Gravelli's response was both exuberant and public. "The creation of the Undersecretariat for the Press and Propaganda, entrusted to Galeazzo Ciano," he told the readers of *Ottobre* in 1935, "is the result for which we have fought." Ciano was evidently the perfect man, being "of our generation," and endowed with those qualities which would enable him to represent "the dynamic element of the European fascist action."[8]

The emergence of Ciano as a key figure in the Fascist Regime was symptomatic of the new direction Mussolini was taking in foreign affairs, and it is significant that when he decided to make a change in the leadership of the Foreign Office in 1936, Ciano would be the man to whom the Duce turned. Yet the significance of individual personalities, even one as dramatic and charismatic as Ciano's, must not be overstated in a transformation of this importance. Coselschi's Action Committees were, after all, created before the establishment of Ciano's Press Bureau. The key, as always, was Mussolini and his continued search for recognition as a leader of a young fascism.

The adherents of the project for a Fascist International were very encouraged by the attitude of the regime, and the creation of Ciano's new office later on reinforced their excitement. Yet no amount of enthusiasm and encouragement from within Italy could substitute for foreign support for the International. From the very beginning, Italian ideas and Italian leadership were tied to cries from outside the peninsula for the creation of the International. Significantly, at the banquet in 1934 which celebrated the founding of the CAUR, at least two non-Italians occupied positions of honor.[9] The first, a certain Giovanni Di Silvestro—representing the *Figli d'Italia* (Sons of Italy) of the United States—paid tribute to Asvero Gravelli, and contributed the startling information that Gravelli was very well known in America. The second foreigner was Simon P. Ooms of Holland, already known to many as a contributor to *Ottobre* and *Antieuropa*. Ooms' ties with official fascist groups in Holland were somewhat cloudy, and his only known connection was with the so-called Black House of Rotterdam, a fascist propaganda center and meeting house. He was evidently associated with the *Front Noir*, or "Black Front," of Holland, but whether he held any official position in its ranks is not known.[10] Ooms' speech, however, represented a certain attitude shared by many fascist movements on the continent. He was concerned about the integrity of national fascism, and stressed the degree to which the International envisaged by the CAUR would guarantee the independence of each particular fascist movement: "Fascism will give every nation its own national pride again. . . . Young Europe will justly be this complex of nations, each one of which, proud of its own race, will give Europe its function in the world."[11]

After this enthusiastic endorsement of the CAUR, Ooms significantly alluded to the Nazi alternative to an International of independent fascisms, grayly remarking that "extreme racial prides, which conceal within them future conflicts, must be avoided."

The concluding speeches at the CAUR banquet were given by the two court philosophers of the movement, Coselschi and Gravelli. (These two, along with Ciano later on, would bear the brunt of the activity on behalf of the creation of a Fascist International.) Coselschi limited his remarks to stressing that the CAUR would be universal, not international (a distinction which would become more significant later), while Gravelli rose to tell his followers that at the moment of the foundation of the International, the memory of the guiding spirit of the movement should be honored: that of Arnaldo Mussolini.[12]

The CAUR, then, represented the first institutionalization of the ideology of universal fascism, and the hopes for the spread of fascist doctrine and the emergence of a fascist Europe rested with Eugenio Coselschi and his various collaborators until Ciano emerged the following year as a figure of prime importance. Coselschi himself revived much of the rhetoric which had been used by D'Annunzio in his picaresque adventure in Fiume more than a decade before, and his constant reiteration of the theme of Imperial Rome would play a major role in his conception of the International. The universality of Rome was conceived in very broad terms, and entailed a kind of syncretism which had been deplored by some of the younger intellectuals mentioned earlier. In 1933 Coselschi dealt with the theme "The Universality of Fascism" in these terms:

> The physical greatness of a city is not enough to establish its true function as a *Capital*, its riches are not enough, its monuments are not enough. One can not dominate forever unless by virtue of an immortal idea, and the force of an inextinguishable civilization.
>
> Now this eternal civilizing and animating mission forms a single unity with the stones, the streets, and the piazzas of Rome. . . .
>
> . . . This unity . . . can only have one name, because this name alone lives and perpetuates itself throughout the centuries, this name alone has been able to resist the centuries.
>
> It is the name of the Past and the Present.
> It is the name of the Future and the Eternal.
> It is the name of the Church and the Empire.
> It is ROME.[13]

The general direction of the CAUR can be seen from these lines. Its aim would be to cull statements of allegiance from various foreign movements calling themselves "fascist," and to integrate these "fascisms" into a loose organization which paid fealty to the genius of Mussolini and the leadership of Italian fascism. Just as the proponents of "young Europe" had stressed that the International would not be an organization of nations, but a unity of movements, the CAUR did not deal with foreign governments but with foreign fascist organizations. As an arm of the government, the CAUR would finance various journals and propagandists, as well as serve as a means for distributing funds to many of the burgeoning philo-fascistic groups on the continent.[14]

The propaganda aims of the CAUR were obviously in direct conflict with the kind of monolithic "International" which would soon be proposed from Berlin, and the tension between fascist Italy and Nazi Germany was clear from the very beginning of the CAUR. Insofar as the CAUR was committed to the independence of local fascisms, it could attack the Nazis both on the grounds of their racial theory (often considered a heresy from the standpoint of Catholic Rome),[15] and on the basis of the expansionist national goals of the *Reich*. Thus, fascist or philo-fascist movements in Catholic countries were more likely to find a friendly reception in Rome than those from Protestant lands, as witness the extended treatment given to the ideas of the young leader of the Spanish Falange, José Antonio Primo de Rivera, in *Ottobre* in 1934.[16] The Spanish leader was extremely impressed by Italian fascism even though he was insistent on the uniqueness of the Falange, and his remarks on the difference between Italy and Germany were very revealing, especially to the readers of the journal for the Fascist International:

> . . . Herein lies the spiritual illumination of the Mussolinian movement. In every country fascism assumes styles and characteristics of its own, which are the circumstantial and local element surrounding the permanent and unique essence of the movement. . . .
> . . . Hitlerism has some essential principles which coincide with our own, but it also has some Germanic and Lutheran characteristics which obviously do not fit in with the Roman idea of

universality, nor the Spanish one, and these principles are summed up in the word "racism."[17]

In the debate between the principles of Rome and Berlin, the propagandists for fascist Italy did not hesitate to stress their own historical primogeniture in the family of civilized peoples. Noting that Charles the Great had found the Germans in a totally barbaric and uncivilized condition, Gravelli ridiculed the ideas of Arthur Rosenberg in May, 1934, and then turned to a discussion of Italy's primacy in the field of modern culture.[18]

This distinction between Rome and Berlin was not lost on the leaders of other European fascist movements, many of whom feared the power of the Nazis, whether or not they found the racist doctrine congenial. If the notion of a Fascist International which permitted individual movements to retain substantial autonomy was an attractive one in the thirties, it would appear to have been a veritable Nirvana to the shattered survivors of European fascism after the Second World War. For example, Horia Sima—Codreanu's successor as the leader of the Rumanian Iron Guard—in his often delirious but highly instructive memoir recalled the CAUR with considerable warmth. His attitude may be considered representative of many of the European fascists in the middle thirties:

> The Duce of fascism sought only spiritual pre-eminence for his doctrine, a recognition by the other movements of the route he had opened up in history. It is his merit to have recognized early the political and spiritual inquietude of the European peoples, and to have found a way of expressing it.
>
> He also realized the necessity for a systematic contract between nationalist movements. To this end he patronized the foundation of the CAUR. . . .[19]

What is crucial here is not the obvious whitewashing of Mussolini's motives, but rather the degree to which the doctrines of universal fascism appealed to leaders of other fascist movements. Léon Degrelle was similarly warm towards the CAUR

and Mussolini during this period. It is hardly surprising to find
Degrelle speaking sympathetically of fascist Rome, since he was
the recipient of considerable financial support from the Duce;
nonetheless, his words during a visit to Rome in the summer of
1936 were notable:

> The Rome of the Caesars and the Popes, liberated, once again
> renewed, is the new symbol of regenerated Italy: youth reveals
> all the forces of history and race, and exalts them in a powerful
> and genuine expansion, which both renews and creates. . . .
>   You Italians and we Rexists, in the act of building a new land,
> raise our spirits by thinking of our mission and the grandeur of
> our task.
>   We also think of our common enemies. . . .[20]

Degrelle had come to Rome under the auspices of the CAUR,
and the rhetoric of his speech shows once again how congenial
the idea of an International of national fascisms was to many
foreign movements. Indeed, the document stipulating the goals
of the CAUR reads much like the propaganda surrounding the
United Nations, calling as it does for world peace and the
development of the talents of each nation, and condemning any
interference in the internal affairs of one nation by another.[21]

The spokesmen for the International were also active in other
similar organizations outside Italy, seizing any opportunity to
beat the drum of their own movement. Thus in November,
1934, we find Gravelli in Vienna at a meeting of the nonfascist,
pacifist *Paneurope* group, led by Count Coudenhouve-Kalerghi.[22]
The subject of the meeting was the world economic crisis, and
Gravelli took the opportunity to deliver the saving gospel
according to Mussolini, reciting the Duce's famous slogan that
the difficulties besetting Europe constituted a crisis of the system
rather than a difficulty within the economic structure, and that
a full-scale transformation of the economic institutions of
Europe was necessary if a final catastrophe was to be avoided.[23]

In the beginning of December, 1934, Gravelli represented Italy at a conference of a group called the "International Action of Nationalisms," a neo-Nazi organization meeting in Zurich.[24] The slogan of this group was: "Nationalists of all countries, unite!", and its membership included representatives of Ireland (General Eoian O'Duffy), England (Oswald Mosley was in Zurich in 1934), Germany (Keller), France (General Pouderoux), Holland (Simon Ooms), and the United States (J. F. Hurst). The International Action of Nationalisms seems to have been financed at least in part by the German Nazis. It met in Berlin in March, 1935, when Gravelli again represented fascist Italy. At the 1934 meeting Gravelli tried to illustrate the differences between fascist and Nazi world-views. Attacking the limitations of racist doctrine, he urged the delegates to remember that each nation had a special mission to fulfill, and that no single monolithic doctrine could possibly permit the various nations of Europe to assemble under its banners. And, in an attempt to weaken the attraction of National Socialist calls to arms, he reminded his listeners that thousands of young men had died for the ideas of Italian fascism, and that the youth of Europe had been entranced by the universal goals of Mussolini.[25]

The fall of 1934 was a busy time for Gravelli. Just a few weeks earlier he had been in Berlin at a meeting of a group called the Society for the Study of Fascism, which met at the Kaiserhof and had an illustrious membership list, including Prince Starhemberg from the *Heimwehr*, the Italian Marchese Antinori, Baron Dr. von Brakel, Dr. Hans Ewers, Otto Freytag, Baron von Manteuffel, and such men of importance in German finance as von Eichborn. The membership of the Society was limited to 143, 82 of whom were "regular" members of the group.[26] The composition of the Society suggests that some elements of the German and Austrian nationalist Right, above all the *Heimwehr*, were seriously interested in cultural collaboration with the Italian fascists.[27] And Gravelli's presence at a gathering of this sort re-emphasizes his role as at least a semi-official representative of the Fascist Regime abroad. Whatever his precise relationship to Palazzo Venezia during this period, it is known that Mussolini made frequent use of journalists in his dealings with the *Reich* in the early thirties,[28] and Gravelli would fit this model. In any case, Gravelli's speeches and writings during the period could hardly have been designed to win the sympathies of the Germans, for he continued to insist upon the ability of fascist movements to develop their own doctrine and their own political style.

We can summarize the movement for a Fascist International, then, as a three-pronged affair. First, an attempt to woo foreign movements by guaranteeing their independence and integrity. Second, a theory of the Corporate State which provided a unique solution to the economic crisis of Europe. Third, a universal, Christian, yet tolerant doctrine which resisted any claims to racial superiority or regional dominance on the continent. All of these elements came into play at the Congress organized by the CAUR at Montreux in December, 1934. This marks the high point of fascist activity on behalf of an International, and offers us a chance to judge the potential for such an organization and the European fascist reaction to it.

At first the Montreux Congress seems to confirm the belief that fascism had won wide support throughout the continent, for no less than thirteen countries were represented. The Austrian *Heimwehr* sent a delegate named Dr. Rimaldini. Belgium was represented by two movements, the *Légion Nationale Belge*, and the *Ligue Corporative du Travail*. Thomas Damsgaard Schmidt, the head of the Danish *National Corpset* attended, as did his countryman Fritz Clausen, representing the Danish National Socialist Party. France was represented by Marcel

Bucard, the head of the *Francistes*, and Greece sent Georges Mercouris, the head of a Social-Nationalist organization. The colorful General Eoian O'Duffy from the Irish Blue Shirts was there, along with Vidkun Quisling of the Norwegian *Nasjonal Samling*, Arnold Meyer of the Dutch *Front Noir*, Eça de Queiroz from Salazar's Portugal, Ion Motza from the Rumanian Iron Guard, and Reutger Essen of the Swedish National Union of Youth. Finally, Jimenez Caballero from the Falange, General Fonjallez from the Swiss Fascist Federation, and M. Tamosciaitis of the Lithuanian Nationalist Party were also present. Significantly, there were no representatives from Nazi Germany.[29]

From the standpoint of the organizers of the Congress, the attendance was encouraging. The main address by Coselschi to the fascists seemed aimed at alleviating any fears they might have had about the role which Mussolini's Italy intended to play, assuring them that *no* nations were formally represented at Montreux, but only parties and movements.[30] For that reason, Coselschi told his listeners, anyone who adhered to the doctrines of the CAUR could join, even if he were not a member of any movement, any party, or any organization. The CAUR was open to all those, he said, who "have their spirit oriented towards the principles of a political, economic, and social renovation, based on the concepts of the hierarchy of the State and the principle of collaboration between the classes."[31] In keeping with the inspiration of those who had initiated the concept of universal fascism, membership was to be a spiritual question, not one of belonging to particular groups. The proper mentality, not the proper pedigree, was to be the main criterion for entry. These assurances were in response to very serious qualms on the part of some of the foreign delegates. As early as September, 1933, Simon Ooms had written in *Ottobre* of his nervousness regarding the CAUR. Ooms feared that it might become a mass organization in which the voices of lesser countries were drowned out by greater powers. He insisted that the CAUR function purely as an organization for the dissemination of ideas.[32] Coselschi was therefore attempting to allay the fears of the delegates before turning to any concrete proposals.

Having assured his audience that Mussolini's Rome desired no suzerainty either at the Congress or within the CAUR, Coselschi went on to guarantee the broadest possible freedom of action for each national element. He stated his dogmatic belief that each nation had to find the solution to its own problems according to its own methods and within its own soul. "I will be," he said, "the most severe and jealous guardian of the national sentiment of each of you."[33]

If each nation was to be permitted to fulfill its own destiny, and if no enforced coordination was to come from Rome, what was to hold the CAUR together? Was there no ideological coherence to the vaunted International? Coselschi turned his attention next to this dilemma, and neatly resolved the difficulty by proclaiming that there was no contradiction in maintaining that fascism was simultaneously national and universal. Fascism's primary point of reference was surely the nation, and as such represented, for Coselschi, the highest development of nationalism in modern times. Yet at the same time, out of the national experience of fascist Italy had emerged certain principles which demonstrated a universal applicability. But unlike the socialists, a fascist need not renounce his own nationality in order to be a true fascist. It was this element which, according to the director of the CAUR, made fascism the true antithesis to Marxism, for the fascists were nationalists in the highest sense, while the Marxists were inevitably internationalists. What was the universality of fascism?

> . . . nothing prevents . . . all our nationalisms from proclaiming the *universality of fascist doctrine* on certain fundamental points

as, for example: *the reconstitution of a State on new bases, of a unified, strong, and disciplined State, the organization of labor; liberties contained within sane and honest limits; installation of order and justice; agreement between social classes; coordinated and solid collaboration between producers. . . .* And so the "super-national" idea harmonizes perfectly with the *national* idea.[34]

The "nationalist" principles were those commonly associated with the Italian Corporate State, and Coselschi made it plain that the "Corporate Idea" was the concept which would lead to a genuine unity of fascist elements in Europe. Further, the vehicle for the transmission of the Corporate faith was to be the youth of Europe. The leader of the CAUR presented his vision of the "fascistization" of Europe to the Congress, a vision which awaited the messianic forces of fascist youth for its fulfillment:

When the youth of Europe, or better yet of the entire world, acquires a revolutionary consciousness in our terms, a consciousness as far from Bolshevik materialism as from individual egotism, then Corporatism will have definitely found the way to conquer the world.[35]

Thus the message of universal fascism found its explicit formulation at the Montreux Congress. The interesting thing about Coselschi's speech was its very positive approach to the difficult question of uniting many diverse movements under a single rubric. The extent to which he was able to stress the common beliefs which united all the groups gathered at Montreux suggests that the kind of Fascist International of youth envisaged by the leader of the CAUR had substantial appeal. This is supported by the attitudes of people such as Horia Sima, long after the failure of the International, as well as by the very positive statements which followed Coselschi's address.

There was virtually unanimous support for the notion of an International which would unite the forces of youth on the continent against the dual enemies of Bolshevik materialism and capitalist egotism.[36] But there was some discussion of the leadership of the International and, as we shall see, a very serious dispute about the role of the Jews in Europe.

As for the leadership of the International, Quisling voiced some concern about the primacy of Rome, and stressed his belief that Rome needed the support of "Nordic civilization."[37] This clumsy reference to Hitler's notable absence from the Montreux Congress set the stage for a fascinating and ultimately decisive debate of the role of the Jews *vis-à-vis* European fascism. The discussion raised the serious issue of the conflict between Rome and Berlin, and exposed the reason for the impossibility of a coherent Fascist International.

The debate itself was initiated by Ion Motza of the Rumanian Iron Guard. He told the delegates that Rumanian Jews had become dominant in his country in the areas of commerce, industry, and the press, and that Jews had heavily infiltrated centers of culture. The Jews, he said, "are a separate group with their own interests and strict solidarity." Motza then went on to demand that the meeting take a position on the Jewish question, on the grounds that Jewish activity was antithetical to the fascist ideal: "The fascist idea, characterized essentially by the desire for order and justice, cannot be realized when one people is dominated by another, as in the case of the Jews in many countries."[38]

The domination of one people by another could take many forms, of course. And, as we have seen from the remarks of Sima and José Antonio, many fascists and philo-fascists might have some sympathy for Italian or German fascism without being willing to be absorbed into an organization dominated by the one or the other. Thus, while Motza was very close to the Nazis in his hatred for the Jews, he might still resist an attempt at Nazi domination of other nations. Furthermore, even those who shared Hitler's conviction that the Jews represented a mortal peril to European societies might be willing to grant other nations the right to deal with their own Jews as they wished, even when that entailed complete equality and toleration. The reactions to Motza's demand that the Congress take a position on the Jewish issue varied widely from country to country, and it is highly instructive to compare these different responses.

The Belgians took an ambivalent position on the question. Paul Hoornaert of the National Legion observed that there were two different kinds of Jew, the "integral" or assimilated Jew, and the "international Jew," the representative of international masonry. The first was to be considered as a responsible citizen of his land; while the second, as a threat to national integrity, ought to be denounced and fought.[39] Somville of the *Ligue Corporative du Travail* agreed with Motza that the Congress ought to make a general statement about the Jews, but felt that the "solution" to the problem might lie in giving the Jews their own land. Consequently, he proposed the possibility of giving Palestine to the Jews so that they could "manifest their own civilization."[40]

Mercouris opposed any attempt to make a general statement about the Jews, arguing that it was a purely internal question, different in each country, and therefore in keeping with the guidelines of the Congress the issue ought to be left to each nation to resolve as it wished.[41] This position was echoed by the spokesmen for Italy, Portugal, and Austria, and the representative of the Austrian *Heimwehr* went so far as to say that in the new Corporate structure of fascist Austria the Jews would be formally represented, along with the representatives of other "autochthonous populations."[42] Wouter Loutkie of the Dutch *Front Noir* openly decried anti-Semitism, but agreed that the question was essentially an internal one for each nation.[43]

The others diverged somewhat from the main thrust of the

argument. Fritz Clausen, speaking for the Danish National Socialists, argued that the Jews were not a nationality but a race, and that therefore the issue was not a national one at all. Further, he observed, echoing the anti-Semitic tones of Ion Motza, the Jews had come to be the symbol for a worldwide materialism, and since fascism represented the forces of an anti-materialist civilization, it must oppose the Jews on all fronts.[44] The Swiss representative, Fonjallez, agreed in principle with Clausen's argument, saying that the nation could not tolerate any foreign force. If the Jews constituted a serious menace to the nation, they must be eliminated.[45]

General O'Duffy observed that there was no Jewish problem in Ireland, but pointed out that only Christians were permitted to join the Blue Shirts.[46] And finally Bucard, who was to become known as one of the most vicious anti-Semites in France in the later thirties, reiterated the general consensus of the Congress, that each nation must act as it judged best and that many countries, such as Italy, had no such problem at all.[47] One of Coselschi's aides, Bartoletto, agreed with Bucard that there was no "Jewish problem" in Italy, observing that of 43 million Italians, a mere 40,000 were Jewish.[48] Yet no *ideological* rejection of anti-Semitism was forthcoming at the Congress from any of the Italians, probably because such a position would have produced an open rupture within the ranks of the delegates. Whatever the reason, it was hardly necessary for anyone further to elaborate a conflict which had already been made crystal clear.

The issue raised by Motza was clearly of considerable significance to the delegates at the Montreux Congress, and presents us with a microcosmic view of the conflicts implicit in any attempt to establish a viable Fascist International. While the anti-Semitism of the Iron Guard was not of the Hitlerian variety, the dominant conflict was between two ideologically opposed views of the world: the Italian fascist conception and the German National Socialist *Weltanschauung*. It was a conflict between those who, like the Nazis, were committed to the defense of the Aryan race, viewed as a supra-national entity, and those who, like the Italians, regarded such notions as mythical nonsense and concentrated on the traditional national units of European society. The interesting thing which emerges from the debate in Montreux is that even those who agreed with the Nazis that the Jews *as a race* constituted a serious menace to Western civilization were also able to agree with the fascists that national integrity precluded a continental solution to the "Jewish problem." Thus, belief in the Nazi notion that the race had to be defended against its corruptors, the Jews, did not necessarily lead to support for the expansion of the German *Reich*.

This is demonstrated by the final resolution on the Jewish issue passed by the Congress. Drafted by Bucard, Somville, and Clausen, the resolution gave full force to the declarations of support for national integrity, and began with a reassertion of the principle that each country had to judge what was best for itself in matters of citizenship, race, and religion. Therefore, the Congress declared that "the Jewish question cannot be dealt with by a universal campaign of hate against the Jews."[49] But, it went on, when the Jews engage in various nefarious activities, fail to contribute to the development of the nation, remain a kind of State within the State, or aid and abet the international revolution so destructive of the ideas of nation and Christian faith, then the Congress "denounces this loathsome action of these elements and undertakes to combat it."[50]

It is not surprising that people with all sorts of differing ideas could be united by their common hatred for Jews, but it *is* significant to note the divergence of ideas within fascist ranks in the middle 1930's. We shall return to this at greater length

in the next chapter; but any claim for the existence of a monolithic fascist ideology in Europe in this period is effectively
dashed by an examination of the debates at Montreux. To the
extent that agreement was possible, it had to be based upon the
Italian conception of a loose association of independent states.
The tie between them was the general belief in the principles
of Italian fascism, that is to say a strong, monolithic, and
hierarchical State, a Corporate structure, and a common desire
for the forces representing Youth to take control of the destiny
of Europe. Thus, the final communique from the Congress
established the conditions of the existence of the International.[51]
First, the relations between the various organizations would be
limited to an exchange of ideas and propaganda. Second, only
those groups would be admitted to membership in the CAUR
who were committed to national revolution, "a revolution
inspired by a true mysticism and an elevated ideal, founded on
Corporativism." Finally, the Congress provided for the creation
of a permanent commission for universal fascism, headed by
Coselschi, Clausen, Bucard, Mercouris, Fonjallez, Quisling,
O'Duffy, and Schmidt. This was to be the Secretariat for the
Fascist International, a supreme coordinating committee for fascist propaganda and communication.

The object of Coselschi and his Italian associates was to
continue to act as a center for fascist propaganda, and to serve
the prestige of Mussolini by gathering statements of support
and adulation for the Italian regime. By continuing to act as a
rallying point for foreign fascist movements, the CAUR could
hope to enhance the position of Italy as a leader in the recon-
struction of Europe, and serve as an inspiration for the younger
generations which, it was firmly believed, would create a fascist
Europe nation by nation. The lack of a rigidly defined criterion
of "true fascism" is evident from the statement issued at the end
of the Montreux Congress by the members of the permanent

commission, inviting the cooperation and participation in its work of

> all those who have participated in this Congress as well as in all the similar movements attached to the fascist and Corporativist idea in all its expressions and under all forms, provided that their action is in accord with the declarations and resolutions approved by the Montreux reunion.[52]

Such a statement was sufficiently broad to include most of the extreme Right in Europe, as well as some traditional Catholic corporate groups. The all-embracing nature of the attempt by the CAUR to serve as a focus of European fascism became even clearer when the commission met for the first time in Paris on January 30, 1935. Those present were Coselschi, Bucard, Quisling, O'Duffy, Schmidt, Mercouris, and Mussert, the head of the Dutch *Nationaal Socialistische Beweging*. The document issued by the commission hailed the mission of fascism as one of peace, of mutual understanding, and of the renovation of peoples and nations. After calling for the systematic coordination of propaganda, which would enable movements to contact each other all over Europe, the commission launched an appeal to the youth of Europe to give its passionate energies to the struggle against materialism, capitalism, and paganism.[53]

Aside from some rhetorical flourishes, the commission at Paris foresaw no particular institutional organization to bind the various fascist movements together. Indeed, this was the next-to-last public gasp of the "Fascist International" which, so far as one can judge, held but one more meeting, organized no further congresses, and made no substantial impact on European affairs.[54] The last recorded meeting, in Amsterdam on April Fool's Day, 1935, was significantly devoted to a critique of racism. The commission condemned "any materialistic concept which exalts the exclusive domination of one race over others."[55] From time to time one finds the CAUR mentioned in terms of some propaganda campaign in some corner of the world, but the great expectations which were associated with the founding of the CAUR were not realized. How does one account for this sudden expiration of an organization which seemed to have had the support of Ciano, the enthusiastic backing of several leading spokesmen for Italian fascism, and the Duce himself? Further, what consequence did the deflation of the campaign for a Fascist International have in terms of Italian foreign and domestic policy in the mid-thirties?

The explanation for the sudden deflation of the CAUR is to be found in a report to Ciano in 1935 from a former schoolmate of his, Dr. Carlo Lozzi.[56] Lozzi was in a unique position to evaluate the impact of the CAUR, since he spoke no less than fourteen languages and had a keen eye for bluff in any tongue. His evaluation of the CAUR is a masterpiece of sarcastic invective, and throws a blinding light on the nature of Coselschi's would-be International.

Lozzi reviewed the history of the CAUR, remarking that the groups had originally received very few members from outside Italy, and had turned to new areas of activity, especially that of posing as the center of a vast international movement:

> To realize this idea of theirs, the CAUR organized . . . an awesome Congress of Universal Fascism, held in the most expensive hotel in Montreux. . . . The CAUR scattered invitations left and right, in order to get the maximum possible number of persons there, since this was the principal aim of the meeting.[57]

The motives of Coselschi and the organizers of the Montreux Congress are painted in very somber tones, suggesting that their previous failure to establish any substantive international ties had forced them to make some kind of show of strength, and that they had brought the group to Montreux more to guarantee the continued support of the CAUR in Italy than out of a serious desire to form a viable international organization.

Further, Lozzi went on, the random invitations produced no end of difficulties and embarrassments for the regime, since many of the delegates represented no party or movement. Reutger Essen, for example, was not a representative from the National Union of Young Swedes, and later stated that he had come to Montreux on his own private initiative. Professor Tamosciaitis had left Montreux and later refused to accept packages of propaganda documents sent to him by the CAUR.

Lozzi continued with scathing denunciations of various other delegates, decrying the Dutch *Front Noir* as an "insignificant and obscure" organization, and noting that Mussolini had barely been saved the embarrassment of having an interview with Arnold Meyer, the head of the group. Lozzi further maintained that Jimenez Caballero had not been at Montreux, despite the claims of the CAUR, and that Primo de Rivera had been very irritated when he saw his name listed as one of the supporters of the Congress.

While the delegates were people of little consequence, the debate at Montreux was substantial, but detrimental to the prestige of the regime: "We will not speak of the Jewish question, raised most inopportunely there, which gave rise to acute dissidence. . . ."

Finally, Lozzi turned his attention to the commission:

Dr. Clausen, head of the Danish Nazi Party, is notoriously the long arm of Hitler in Denmark, and is abundantly financed by him: however, thanks to the CAUR he is a member of a committee for fascist coordination!

Bucard . . . is a noted pederast. . . .

Mr. Thomas Damsgaard Schmidt is the head of a Danish Party which exists only in his own mind: he has no following in Denmark, where he is perfectly unknown. . . .

. . . The Commission is a brazen bluff. . . .

For Ciano's analyst, then, the CAUR represented a gigantic hoax. Coselschi, rather than organizing an international propaganda network of the sort Ciano had envisaged for the aggrandizement of the regime (and of his own person), had gotten the regime involved with a group of fascist, pseudo-fascist, and neo-fascist entrepreneurs, involved in the enterprise of soliciting funds from Rome for their own diversion and advancement. The inference from all of this was clear: Coselschi and his associates did not know the difference between a true fascist and a *poseur*:

> . . . given their ridiculous organization, and thus also the phe-nomenal ignorance of their directors, they enter into relations with movements that have nothing in common with fascism. . . .

For Lozzi, the foreign movements with whom the CAUR were dealing were not in the least interested in participating in a great work of fascist indoctrination, but only in Italian lire.

This report explains the otherwise perplexing contraction of the activities of the CAUR following the Montreux Congress. There seems to be little reason to doubt that Ciano had soured on the organization, and decided to drastically cut back the scope of its operations. We might note in passing that Ciano continued to have trouble explaining the "true" content of fascism to Coselschi, who evidently failed to realize that anti-Semitism was something to be studiously avoided. In January, 1936, Coselschi wrote to Ciano to ask whether contacts should be continued with the Rumanian Iron Guard, citing a letter from Motza offering to send food parcels to Italian troops in Africa. Motza had unleashed one of his typically wordy attacks on the "international Jewish conspiracy," claiming that "all of our Jews anticipated, and still anticipate with almost mystical passion, the downfall of fascism and the ruin of the Duce fol-lowing the attacks by the Masons and the English."[58] Ciano scribbled a terse "No" at the bottom of the letter.

The Lozzi report, exposing the shabbiness of Coselschi's operation, is significant for two reasons. In the first place, it shows that the attempt to organize a Fascist International had been ineptly managed and conducted with surprising gullibility and naïveté. This helps to account for the restraints imposed upon the CAUR after Montreux, and for the highly critical attitude taken by Ciano towards the organizers of the Congress. Secondly, Lozzi's remarks about the actual course of the debates at Montreux tell us a good deal about the criteria employed by the Italian regime to distinguish between those movements it considered "fascist" and those it did not. In particular, it is important to note that anti-Semites were not taken to be good fascists, and philo-Nazis were downgraded as agents of Hitler (and hence presumably poor candidates for recruitment to "fascist" ranks). From Lozzi's point of view, then, neo-Nazi movements had "nothing in common with fascism," and should not have been included at the Montreux Congress.

Yet despite the paucity of results produced by the Montreux reunion, it is important to an understanding of both Italian and European fascism. The debates at Montreux illustrate the conflicts within a movement which many have taken to be highly unified, and at the same time they help us recognize those themes which were actually shared by most, if not all, of the movements which called themselves "fascist" in the early thirties. Foremost among these themes is the *leitmotif* already discussed so frequently here—that fascism was the embodiment of the forces of Youth in the West.

Even some of the CAUR's former friends were disillusioned by the course of events, albeit for different reasons from those held by the leaders in the seats of power in Rome. Following his brief appearance at the inaugural banquet of the CAUR, Asvero Gravelli had been notably absent from the functions of the organization of which he had presumably been a prime mover. Excluded from the formal structures of the

CAUR, not invited to the Montreux Congress, and not even mentioned in the propaganda activities proposed by the Paris Commission, Gravelli and his followers voiced their frustration and anger at the CAUR early in 1935, observing that they had been left out of an organization they had created.[59] Indeed they *had* been excluded, and furthermore their own views on the universality of fascism, based upon an extreme tolerance for regional and national variations on the basic Corporate theme, were fast being repudiated by the leaders of the International. On January 1, 1935, a group of those who had been present at Montreux met in Rome to establish an international center for Corporate studies.[60] The list of names is clearly indicative of their ideological predilections: O'Duffy, Meyer, Loutkie, and Fonjallez. These represented the reactionary, ultramontanist elements of the International, and appropriately enough they found their institutional support in Rome not from the CAUR, but rather from a group called *Italia e fede* (Italy and Faith), a Catholic center and publishing house.[61]

This brings us back to one of the important elements in the discussions at Montreux which has significant implications on the Italian domestic scene: the theory of Corporative universality. The establishment of the Center for Corporate Studies outside the sphere of CAUR control indicates that theories of the Corporate State were still controversial within Italy. The contending elements were many indeed, and an analysis of this question would take us far afield. It is important to note, however, that the very concept of a Corporate State involved problems which brought the relationship between Church and State into question, and that several spokesmen for the Vatican were not prepared to leave this field entirely open to the intellectual formulations of secular theorists. The *Italia e fede* group was simply one of the most important Catholic organizations attempting to maintain a strong Catholic influence over the

development of Corporate theory,[62] especially since there
seemed to be a strong possibility in the early thirties that a
genuinely profound restructuring of the State might take
place.[63]

The resolution passed at the Montreux Congress was general
enough that no group need have felt threatened by the idea of
an international Corporatist movement. But the foundation of
the international center under the aegis of *Italia e fede* indicates
that the Catholic-secular tension existed on the international
level as well as within Italy, and that this tension had produced
a cleavage within the ranks of delegates at Montreux. Those
who supported the *Italia e fede* would have a far less radical
concept of the Corporate transformation of society than, for
example, the supporters of Giuseppe Bottai.

This division over the nature of the Corporate State was a
further blow to the supporters of universal fascism, and disillu-
sionment with the CAUR was not long in coming. Weakened
by the devastating picture of its activities which Ciano had
received, alienated from Gravelli's group, and torn by internal
debates over the nature of Corporatism, the CAUR gradually
faded into the background of Italian politics.

Of the groups we have discussed within Italy, the only one
which continued enthusiastic support of the CAUR after the
spring of 1935 was that around Oddone Fantini and his journal,
Universalità Fascista.[64] In February, Fantini pledged uncondi-
tional support for the CAUR, and as late as June, 1935, we
find him reporting enthusiastically that the *Légion Nationale*
in Brussels had opened an exhibition of Universal Fascism, and
that the CAUR had received a position of honor in the exhibition.[65] Not surprisingly, it seems that Fantini's stock with the
regime had fallen to a low level indeed. In an unsigned report
sent to Mussolini in the winter of 1933, the Duce's informer
dealt with developments surrounding the Fascist Institutes of

Culture, in particular the Institute in Rome, which Fantini directed:

> . . . [the Roman Institute] has been given to the *medaglia d'oro* Fantini, who enjoys a very meager moral reputation, and who headed a certain institute of a Corporative nature, of miniscule scientific importance. . . . [giving the Institute to Fantini] has produced a very damaging impression. . . .[66]

So the groups dedicated to the promulgation of universal fascism were under heavy criticism in Rome by the turn of the year 1935. It is not surprising that when *Antieuropa* returned to normal publication in January, 1936, after a number of special issues, the subtitle, "Review of Fascist Expansion in the World" had been dropped from its masthead. At the same time, the criticism of Nazi racism, previously endemic in its pages, decreased substantially.[67]

This is not to say that the rhetoric associated with the expansion of fascism vanished from the fascist press. But the "movement" henceforth was channeled into more official guidelines, and brought under control of the Party. As Zangrandi acutely observes, the problem for young Italians seeking to establish contact with other young intellectuals abroad interested in universal fascism was to avoid the stultifying control of the Party hierarchs, especially those connected with GUF.[68]

Mussolini was certainly eager to continue his cultivation of European youth, and young Europeans were generous in their acclaim of the Italian dictator. In May, 1935, for example, Mussolini received the directors of the International Confederation of Students, among whom were the president of the *"Pax Romana"* (worldwide organization of Catholic students) and the president of the Federation of Jewish Students. These young men declared their admiration for Mussolini's achievements, saying that they recognized the Duce as "the spiritual head of youth."[69] Mussolini could have asked for no greater adulation.

Yet it is important that demonstrations of this sort were increasingly under Party control, rather than being left to the inspiration of youth itself.

For its part, the regime had evidently become convinced that fascist expansion was not a task to be entrusted to amateurs, and that such funds as were dispersed to foreign fascisms ought to be supervised by more responsible elements than the entrepreneurs of the CAUR and other such organizations. Thus, Mussolini was extremely active in financing various European fascist groups, and especially the Austrian *Heimwehr*. Further, the funds distributed seemed, by and large, to be aimed at the containment of Nazi Germany.[70]

We have seen repeated evidence of the hostility of the regime toward the Nazis, and yet we know that by 1936 Mussolini was beginning to work towards a *rapprochement* with the German *Reich*.[71] Such a turnabout in fascist foreign policy could not help but have profound effects upon the political and cultural scene in Italy. As we have suggested earlier, there was always an intimate connection between domestic and foreign policy under Mussolini, and the fundamental change in Italy's relationship with Hitler entailed changes within Italy. The development of the Axis between Hitler and Mussolini made the continued existence of a movement for the creation of a Fascist International highly problematic, especially since the International had been conceived as a movement outside the control of any great national power. A great many other developments jeopardized the International, but the increasing warmth between the two dictators was of paramount importance.

In addition to these changes in foreign policy, there was a "cultural shock" associated with the formation of the Axis. One can readily imagine the effect this new alliance had on young fascists who had passionately defended the originality and uniqueness of Italian fascism *vis-à-vis* the "barbaric" and "Cel-

tic" doctrines from beyond the Alps. Further, the impending
alliance with Germany meant a drastic reappraisal of the entire
notion of racism, and indeed ultimately entailed the adoption of
anti-Semitic legislation in Italy itself.

Thus, within five years the advocates of universal fascism had
gone from the creation of the CAUR to the rejection not only
of their institutions, but indeed of the very essence of their
world-view. How did they react to this defeat? For this bizarre
story it is necessary to step back for a moment from the detailed
investigation of the doctrine of universal fascism, and consider
one of its central problems: the "Jewish question."

CHAPTER FIVE

Beyond the International

∧∧∧ The effort to construct a Fascist International on the basis of an ideology of Corporatism and the cult of Youth failed in the middle thirties. The greatest single reason for its failure was the new direction of fascist foreign policy, and we shall deal with that change and its implications shortly. But there were many other contributing factors to the collapse of the movement. The Lozzi report demonstrated the incompetence of the leadership from Italy promoting the International, as well as the flimsiness of the foreign organizations and movements which were to have provided its backbone. Furthermore, the dispute over the "Jewish question" at Montreux shows that there were serious doctrinal differences which made any durable union of national fascisms highly tenuous. This was to be demonstrated more concretely later on by the Axis alliance, a union which was a highly personal one between the two dictators, and which was never based on any solid unity of vision between Nazi Germany and fascist Italy.[1]

The fundamental reason for the collapse of the movement for a Fascist International remains the change in Italian foreign policy in the thirties. Mussolini's increasingly active involvement abroad, first in Ethiopia, then in Spain, meant that propaganda activities had to be coordinated with Italian foreign adventures rather than moving freely in the recruitment of declarations of support from other fascisms. And the necessity of training troops and mobilizing support for foreign wars understandably drained off energy and personnel from many enterprises, so that the movement to create a Fascist International suffered greatly from a shortage of manpower. Such important figures as Giuseppe Bottai, Vittorio Mussolini, and Asvero Gravelli departed for foreign theaters of action, leaving their groups without effective leadership.

Finally, the increasing interrelation between Mussolini and Hitler meant that anti-Nazi polemics in the Italian press had to be suppressed, and with the emergence of Italian anti-Semitism in 1936, 1937, and 1938 the very basis of fascist doctrine had to be re-evaluated in the light of Mussolini's new attitude towards racism. It was no longer possible, in the second half of the decade, to present Italian fascism as an ideological alternative to German National Socialism, since the two countries were acting in concert and Mussolini had moved to a position of considerable support for the Nazi doctrines.

The effect of these various changes was to isolate many of those who had worked for a Fascist International. In particular, the adoption of anti-Semitism by the regime produced a cultural trauma of major proportions within the ranks of Italian youth and Italian culture. For many of those who had supported the doctrines of universal fascism, the adoption of the anti-Semitic laws of 1938 provided the occasion for a break with fascism itself, and drove them into open opposition to Mussolini.[2] For others, the crisis produced by the changed doctrines of the regime lured them into an adoption of racism. Whatever the particular result, 1936 marked a major turning point in the history of Italian fascism.

Most historians of the fascist *Ventennio* are agreed that the adoption of the anti-Semitic legislation in the late thirties produced a genuine rupture in Italian society.[3] Until that period, Mussolini had enjoyed a high degree of personal popularity.

Even those dissident elements we have examined could feel a strong sense of identification with Mussolini at the same time that they criticized many of the failures of the Fascist Regime. As we have seen, it was possible to believe that fascism would eventually carry out a genuine social revolution, even though it was clear throughout the history of the regime that that revolution had not yet occurred. This was especially true in those segments of society which enjoyed a certain freedom of expression in the press.

The change in fascist doctrines which culminated in the racial laws of 1938 produced a "crisis of conscience" among those elements which had genuinely been committed to a "Fascist Revolution." For Ruggero Zangrandi, the anti-Semitic laws marked the beginning of a new period in fascist history: "It was then that the second part of the voyage across fascism began for those [youth]: to be liberated from it, that is to say, to find a way to oppose it, or to fight it."[4]

For Zangrandi and those who would follow him into opposition to the Fascist Regime, the fascist practice could no longer be accommodated within an ideology which called for "revolutionizing" fascism. The adoption of anti-Semitism by the hierarchs of fascism was something these young Italians found too foreign and too offensive to be tolerated. And whereas in the past unattractive doctrines had been attributed to those around Mussolini, Italian "racism" was too clearly associated with the Duce himself to be explained away. To fully understand the shock which Mussolini's adoption of anti-Semitism produced, we must look at the relations between Jews and Gentiles in Italy preceding the 1938 legislation, and in particular at Mussolini's attitude toward the "Jewish question."

The Jews of Italy had been unusually fortunate in their relations with their Christian countrymen, for Italy had very little of the mass anti-Semitism which characterized much of

Europe in the early twentieth century. Between 40,000 and 60,000 Jews lived in Italy and the Empire during the *Ventennio*, or roughly one-tenth of 1 per cent of the total national population. Their impact—as the impact of a specifically Jewish community—was as marginal as their total number. From the middle of the eighteenth century on, Italian Jews had been able to function on a level of increasing parity with their Gentile countrymen, and the assimilation of Jews into Italian life on both the legal and psychological levels went forward with increasing tempo and success.

Indeed, this assimilation was pronounced. Figures on mixed marriages, gathered from the Jewish archives, reveal that from 1930 to 1937 30 per cent of Jews who married chose members of other faiths. This remarkable figure compares with 11 per cent in Germany and 14 per cent in Hungary.[5]

Italians, then, were quite willing to deal with their Jewish compatriots on equal terms—by accepting them into their families. And the Italian Jews were equally prepared to abandon their purely Jewish identities for participation in Italian life. In fact it might be argued that the Jewish community of Italy had embarked upon a course of assimilation with such great enthusiasm and success that had it not been for the anti-Semitic legislation of 1938–43, it might almost have vanished completely. Luigi Luzzatti, a journalist in the late 1930's, says: "I was born a Jew, and I return passionately to being one whenever I am criticized for being Jewish or my being Jewish puts me in danger . . . if anti-Semitism ended I would publicly proclaim my Christianity."[6]

As one might expect, the Jews themselves felt a strong sense of patriotism and loyalty towards Italy. Mussolini personally recognized the substantial contributions of the Jews to Western civilization, and indeed frequently remarked to his friends that the Jews were the only people in the history of the world to have given a God to humanity. On the subject of any intrinsic distinction between Jew and Gentile, he was categoric: "In Italy there is absolutely no difference between Jew and non-Jew in all fields, in religion, in politics, in the military, in economics. . . ."[7]

Assimilated as they were, many Jews were to be found within the fascist ranks. In 1922 there were nearly 750 Jews in the Fascist Party; by 1928 an additional 1,770 had joined; and by 1933 yet another 4,800. Like all other Italians, the Jews saw a variety of tendencies at work in the Fascist Regime. What they saw most clearly, however, was that the situation of the Jews got better and better over the first decade of fascist rule. They consequently behaved pragmatically when they supported a government which not only improved their legal status but, as we shall see, also became for a time one of the foremost advocates of the Zionist cause in Europe.

The middle period of fascism, which saw the consolidation of the Fascist Regime, brought about an increasingly warm and mutually beneficial relationship between the regime and the Italian Jews. Not only were the Jews given a new and coherent legal status, but in the area of foreign policy Mussolini was making increasingly pro-Zionist noises. A striking example of this is the meeting between Chaim Weizmann and Mussolini in the Quirinale in September, 1926. During the course of the discussions Mussolini expressed sympathy for the Zionist cause, suggesting that Italy might well be able to provide the assistance which the British had thus far failed to deliver.[8] This was not, as many suspected at the time, just another of Mussolini's rhetorical flourishes. It was rather a genuine statement of the dictator's beliefs. Not only was he sympathetic to the plight of the Jews, but he was intensely interested in establishing Italian influence over the Mediterranean, and Zionism was something he could exploit toward this end. The meeting with Weizmann was only the first in a long series of meetings with Zionist leaders. The following June he met with Victor Jacobson, a representative of the Zionist "executive," and in October with Nachum Sokolov. With this last meeting, Mussolini became lionized by Zionism. Sokolov not only praised the dictator's human qualities, but announced his firm belief that fascism was immune from anti-Semitic preconceptions. He went even further. In the past, Sokolov observed, there might have been uncertainty about the true nature of fascism; but now, "we begin to understand its true nature . . . true Jews have never fought against you."[9]

These words, tantamount to a Zionist endorsement of the Fascist Regime, were echoed in Jewish periodicals all over the world. In this period, expressions of loyalty and affection for fascism poured out of the Jewish centers of Italy. In its turn, the regime was quick to act, arranging that public examinations should not fall on Jewish holy days, and making generous arrangements for the rights of the Jewish community.[10]

At the time of the Concordat with the Vatican, the Fascist Regime had found it necessary and desirable to formalize relations with the Jewish community as well, and the keynote for the new system was struck by Mussolini in a speech to the Chamber on May 13, 1929:

> We respect this sacred character of Rome. But it is ridiculous to think, as has been said, that the synagogues must be closed.... Jews have been in Rome from the times of the kings . . . there were 50,000 at the time of Augustus, and they asked to cry on the corpse of Julius Caesar. They will remain undisturbed.[11]

Thus any anti-Semitic elements in Italy in the early thirties had to contend with the explicit statement by the Duce that the Jews were to be treated like other Italians. In fact, this period saw a veritable outpouring of philo-Semitic writings, often from the most surprising sources. Even Farinacci, who would become one of the blackest racists after 1937, came to restrict anti-Semitic articles in his journal; in July, 1930, he published a long, vicious attack on racism and Nazi anti-Semitism.[12] On February 25, 1929, Costanzo Ciano visited the Temple of Livorno and said that there were too few Jews in Italy.[13]

Thus, by the time of the Montreux Congress, there was nothing vaguely resembling a "Jewish question" in Italy, a fact recognized by people like Bucard at the Congress itself. This set fascist Italy in clear contrast with Hitler's Germany, and indeed the early relations between Hitler and Mussolini illustrate the conflict which existed over this issue. After his first conversation with Hitler in Venice in 1934, Mussolini was reported to have told a friend that "it is not possible to talk with an idiot."[14] This simply confirmed the impression that the Duce had acquired a year earlier, when Mussolini sent the German *Führer* a message suggesting a lessening of German anti-Semitic policies and propaganda. On that occasion Mussolini had even gone so far as to point out the lunacy of Nazi anti-Semitism:

> Every regime has not only the right but the duty to eliminate from posts of command those elements not completely trust-worthy, but for this it is not necessary, indeed it can be noxious, to carry to the level of race—Aryanism and Semitism—what is rather simply a measure of defense and the development of revolution.[15]

This (as we have seen) was the position finally adopted by the representatives at Montreux, a position which skirted the issue of "race" by leaving each national fascism free to deal with its internal problems as it saw fit. Hitler's response to these words of revolutionary advice was heated. He told Mussolini's representative that the Italians did not understand the Jews, and that the course of the German revolution must be in the hands of Aryans. Racism, for Hitler, was not subject to negotiation.[16]

This clash presented Mussolini with a serious problem. Bombarded by many of the most authoritative spokesmen of Italian culture (including spokesmen for a Fascist International) requesting that he dissociate himself entirely from Nazi doctrines, yet unwilling to break off relations altogether with the only other government in Europe to call itself "fascist," Mussolini tried for a while to steer a middle course. On the one hand he let it be known that he was sympathetic to the plight of the German Jews and would do much to help them (Weizmann said in May, 1933, that Mussolini would not oppose plans to transfer German Jews to Palestine).[17] On the other hand, he became convinced that he could do little to deter the Nazis from their course of persecution. His activities for the next several years would be directed towards the dual attempt to moderate the intense anti-Semitism of the Nazis whenever possible while trying to circumscribe Hitler's sphere of activity. As late as 1937 this policy would be evident, when Mussolini advised Schuschnigg to accept "collaboration" with the Nazis while simultaneously urging the Austrians not to adopt the anti-Semitic policies of the *Reich*.[18]

The five-year period from 1932 to 1937 saw Mussolini maintain his public position on the "Jewish question." Thus, for example, he authorized Angelo Sacerdoti, the Chief Rabbi of Rome, to take a strong anti-Nazi stance at the World Jewish Congress in August, 1933. With the explicit support of the Duce, Sacerdoti spoke of Judaism and the civilization of Rome as forces which had formed the modern world, forces which ought to work in harmony with each other. He further proposed a resolution against Nazi racism.[19]

Having said all this, however, it must be noted that Mussolini was simultaneously trying to ingratiate himself with the rulers in Berlin. At the same time that he was advising both his own Embassy in Berlin and various Jewish organizations that Italy would accept any Jewish emigrant from Germany (provided that he was not an enemy of the Nazi regime),[20] he was extracting guarantees from Jewish organizations that they would not press their attacks against Hitler if Italy could succeed in gaining some modification of the Nazis' anti-Semitic posture. In addition, Mussolini had established contacts with some of the more active centers of German nationalism early in his own regime, and he had continued to try to win the support of rightist elements in Germany on behalf of Italy's demands for revision of the Versailles Treaties.[21] The international events of the middle thirties combined to accentuate the pro-German elements in the patchwork quilt of Mussolini's foreign policy, as did the significant change in leadership within the Foreign Office itself.

The failure of Mussolini's *Patto a Quattro* (Four Power Pact), and the lack of any tangible support from France and England for his defense of the Austrian regime against the attempted Nazi *putsch* in 1934, led the Italians to reconsider some of the basic tenets of their European policies. This is not the place to undertake a detailed examination of European affairs in the thirties, but it is necessary to stress the extent to which Mussolini felt himself isolated by the English and the French, and the transformation of Italian foreign policy in the mid-thirties was no doubt to a large extent due to this feeling. Above all, the change in the entourage which advised the Duce on foreign problems must be stressed, for in a personal dictatorship those who advise the single ruler gain a disproportionate influence over a nation's destiny.

The member of the Foreign Office who, above all others, represented the traditional Italian policy of striving to guarantee an independent Austrian buffer between Italy and Germany was Fulvio Suvich. In a note to Mussolini a few months before his removal from office in the summer of 1936, Suvich repeated his

firm conviction that "it would be an illusion to believe that
Germany, having arrived at the Brenner . . . would stop . . ."[22]
He counseled the dictator to reassure the other powers of
Europe that the momentary closeness between Italy and Germany in 1936, produced primarily by the sanctions against Italy
stemming from the fascist invasion of Ethopia, was not to be
viewed as indicating a new course in Italian policy but simply
as a momentary expedient. For Suvich the idea of an alliance
with Germany was unthinkable, and his replacement by Ciano
in the summer of 1936 was a clear omen of the changing course
of the Duce's thinking, a change which was to have domestic
reverberations of the first order.[23]

The entry of Ciano into the Foreign Office was an event of
considerable significance in the evolution of fascist policy, both
at home and abroad. Ciano himself believed that his leadership
had finally made the Foreign Office "fascist" for the first time,
and that henceforth Italian foreign affairs would reflect the
"new" mentality of the epoch.[24] However, in concrete terms
Ciano's stewardship saw the evolution of the Axis, an alliance
which he would finally come to oppose, but for which he must
nonetheless bear the lion's share of responsibility. Since Ciano
was a figure who represented the "new man" for so many fascists, the crisis within Italian fascism produced by the alliance
with the Nazis was heightened; those who otherwise would
have condemned the Axis now had to sever their emotional ties
to Ciano himself as well as reject the alliance. Many adopted
anti-Semitism when confronted by this crisis, while others would
turn to explicitly anti-fascist actions when the racial laws were
promulgated. The important fact here is that the adoption of the
anti-Semitic laws by the regime, coupled with the personal
involvement of both Mussolini and Ciano in the evolution of
this policy, made the issue emotionally charged in a way it
would not have been had these policies not been so closely tied
to two charismatic figures.

It is surprising, in retrospect, that the anti-Semitic laws met with so little resistance from within the regime, for most of the members of the Fascist Grand Council were opposed to their adoption.[25] This holds true even for those who had been anti-Semitic for many years, like Emilio De Bono, who recognized that anti-Semitism would be viewed as something foreign to most Italians.[26] Further, if we can believe the former head of the Secret Police, Mussolini was advised that the racist legislation would most likely produce serious resistance throughout the country, a prediction amply borne out in the late thirties and forties.[27]

But the maturation of the alliance with Hitler did not permit Mussolini to equivocate about Italian anti-Semitism, for it was simply not possible for the Axis to have any coherence if Italy continued to be opposed to the fundamental tenet of Nazi ideology. The primary cause of Italian anti-Semitism was the alliance with Hitler, not because of any direct pressure from the Nazis (there was none until 1943), but because of the logic of the alliance itself.[28] In sum, these policies were adopted in spite of known opposition to them, and Ciano was a key figure in their development.

We can now appreciate the depth of the crisis which this produced among Italians who had worked for the development of a "revolutionary" fascism that would become the model for a reinvigorated Europe, especially those who had viewed men like Ciano and Bottai as their spokesmen in the higher levels of the fascist hierarchy. Having expended so much energy to demonstrate the incompatibility of Nazism and Italian "universal" fascism, they found themselves confronted by a regime which adopted the very policies the proponents of universal fascism had condemned for years. Further, the adoption of the anti-Semitic measures was greeted with widespread hostility among the Italian populace, stemming as it did from foreign sources, and appearing in a country which not only had no tradition of mass anti-Semitism but which had opposed those doctrines for decades.

The response to this dilemma was, as we said earlier, a varied one. For those who, like Asvero Gravelli, were personally close to Mussolini, deep loyalty to the person of the Duce enabled them to surmount this "crisis of conscience."[29] Gravelli remained dedicated to Mussolini to the bitter end, and recanted his earlier proclamation as a prophet of the "protestants of the religion of racism." In an article suggestively entitled *"Il razzismo italiano tra l'universalismo astratto e l'universalità concreta"* (Italian Racism Between Abstract Universalism and Concrete Universality) written in 1938,[30] Gravelli not only endorsed Italian racism, but took pains to claim that this doctrine was not part of a European-wide phenomenon but rather a uniquely Italian development which stood for "universal" tendencies. Thus he was able to maintain the position which had been adopted by the Montreux Congress, for Gravelli argued that each people would develop its own version of racism, and defend itself according to its own national traditions and inclinations.

Interestingly enough, Gravelli's adoption of racism did not prevent him from continuing his journalistic and personal activities on behalf of the expansion of fascism in the world and the spread of the cult of Youth. In the middle and late thirties he became associated with the *Istituto Europa Giovane* (Young Europe Institute) in Rome,[31] which published a monthly periodical entitled *Nazionale*. The director of this Institute, Pietro Gorgolini, was a fascist of long standing, and he devoted the activities of the Institute to spreading fascist values throughout the peninsula and to acquainting his followers with foreign developments of importance to fascist culture. When racism became the order of the day Gorgolini quickly joined the new movement, and organized a conference on Nazi literature in

1938. The Institute also published several books and pamphlets, ranging from works by Arnaldo Mussolini to topics related to the old notion of universal fascism, such as "The Rejuvenation of Europe." In addition to Gravelli, Gorgolini had managed to attract some of the leading fascist intellectuals to the Institute, such as Emilio Bodrero and Paolo Orano, and such foreign luminaries as Corneliu Codreanu and Mihail Manoilesco from the Rumanian Iron Guard, Armand Godoy from the Falange, and Franz Arens from Germany.[32]

This sort of activity, characteristic of the supporters of universal fascism, was no longer as valued by the regime as it had been in the early thirties, and financial support for Gorgolini's Institute was removed in 1941, when the Ministry of Popular Culture closed it down.[33]

While personal loyalty and affection for Mussolini might explain Asvero Gravelli's adoption of anti-Semitism, the case of Giuseppe Bottai is more complex and, in terms of the problems we have been dealing with, far more significant. For Bottai's anti-Semitism was evidently a virulent and deeply felt expression. Even the cynical Ciano marveled at the heat of Bottai's expressions on the "Jewish question,"[34] and while the response of most Italians to the racial laws was apathetic (if not antagonistic), Bottai eagerly embraced the new doctrine as a method of finally creating the "new fascists" which had been his concern for more than fifteen years. The means for the creation of these new people was, as always, education:

> In the elementary school, by means suited to the infant level, a climate will be created that is appropriate for the formation of a first embryonic racist conscience, while in the *scuola media* the highest mental development of the adolescents, already in contact with the humanistic tradition . . . will make it possible to establish the bases of racist doctrine, its ends and its limits. The propagation of the doctrine will continue, finally, in the

scuola superiore, where studious youth . . . can prepare itself to be, in its own turn, the animator and teacher [of racism]. . . .[35]

Bottai, as Minister of Education during the racist period, was in an excellent position to enforce the adoption of anti-Semitic doctrines, and his zealous conversion to the racist faith is eloquent testimony to the attractiveness of that doctrine, at least to some fascists. In Bottai's case, the question is complicated by his highly critical attitude towards the regime, for he had acquired a justly deserved reputation as the "frondist" within the fascist camp. As we have seen, young Italians were great supporters of Bottai, and his stance on the "Jewish question" is a measure of the depth of the crisis produced by the change in fascism in the late thirties. Bottai seems to have embraced anti-Semitism as a genuinely effective way of bringing about a change within the heart of fascism.

It is always dangerous to try to evaluate men's motives, yet in this case Bottai's intentions are most important. It has been suggested that his actions between 1938 and 1940 were the result of a considerable amount of autonomy granted him by Mussolini, in an attempt to win over the majority of Italian youth to the fascist cause.[36] If it is true that Bottai had achieved this degree of freedom, it might be argued that his anti-Semitism was a mask for his activities, which were directed toward the substitution of his own brand of fascism for Mussolini's. Ruggero Zangrandi has suggested that Bottai was aiming toward "creating a personal political base, looking towards the succession, resting on the undoubtedly superior part of Italian culture, and on elements which he knew very well were anti-fascist."[37]

If Bottai was seriously engaged in such subversive activities, an attitude of trenchant anti-Semitism would have served him well as a defense against charges of subversion from other Party hierarchs. Whatever the truth may be, it is beyond question that Bottai continued to act for the creation of his own kind of fascism, and under the rubric of his anti-Semitic outcries in the late thirties he continued to hold conferences on universal fascism for many young fascists. (Indeed, many of the meetings sponsored by the government for young fascist intellectuals continued to revolve around themes of universal fascism, even as Italy moved ever closer to Hitler's fatal embrace.)[38] Bottai's publishing ventures in the late thirties and early forties, in particular his new journal *Primato* (*Primacy*, 1940) attracted many of those most highly critical of the regime to his side, and the participation of such genuine anti-fascists as Giorgio Spini and Luigi Salvatorelli leaves little doubt as to the direction of Bottai's activities.[39]

Whether or not Bottai's anti-Semitism was a mask for his attempts to promote his own version of fascism, the outcome of his maneuver was disastrous for his program to stimulate an independent school of fascist thought and action in Italy. Once the Axis was established and war had begun in Europe, there was no hope for such ventures as Bottai had in mind. Surprisingly, he was highly optimistic about the possibility of Italian cultural supremacy in a Europe conquered by the Axis.[40] His own activities after the formation of the Axis were aimed at maintaining a certain public support for ideas which had previously been embodied in the universal fascism movement, hoping that they could be successfully institutionalized after the war.

The ironic tragedy of this attitude is that, once the alliance with Hitler became established, both Bottai and Ciano found themselves in agreement on the universal relevance of Italian fascism, and on the odious nature of the Axis.[41] Yet both had contributed mightily to the formation of the Axis and the acceptance of anti-Semitism. Their optimism on the role that the Italian genius and the innovatory forces of Italian youth might play in the Europe of the future was as misguided as their failure to oppose the racial policies in Italy when first proposed.

When we turn from these two pivotal figures in the history of fascism to the more human-sized personalities involved in the movement for universal fascism, we find a monotonous conformity to the will of Mussolini. The CAUR, once in the forefront for the creation of a new world fascist movement, became one of many centers for the dissemination of racist literature, and a conduit for Italian funds to foreign movements congenial to the regime.[42] From 1938 to the end of the war, the CAUR would be primarily concerned with the distribution of literature on behalf of anti-Semitism and other neo-Nazi doctrines. Its final incarnation was in the form of a journal called *Giovane Europa* (*Young Europe*), which was a mere parrot for Nazi slogans.[43]

Oddone Fantini and the group around *Universalità Fascista* continued to act as if the day of Italian international hegemony was about to dawn; but calls for the creation of a Fascist International vanished by 1936, and the once prevalent attacks on Nazi doctrines vanished altogether.[44] Fantini never became one of the vociferous advocates of anti-Semitism, but in the summer of 1937 *Universalità Fascista* published an article on National Socialist demographic politics which praised Nazi efforts to increase the German birth rate and remove undesirable elements from the population, citing the Nuremburg racial laws favorably.[45]

The School of Fascist Mysticism became one of the principal propaganda organizations for the regime in the late thirties, and innumerable conferences, radio broadcasts, movies, and lectures on the "Jewish question" were produced under its auspices, culminating in an attempt to integrate anti-Semitism into the fabric of "fascist mysticism."[46]

The actions of these various individuals and groups is sufficient to demonstrate that the adoption of racism was not incompatible with the belief that a "revolutionary" fascism might yet provide the leadership which Europe so desperately needed. Renzo De Felice, speaking of those young fascists who accepted anti-Semitism, supports this position:

> [The adoption of anti-Semitism] must be viewed as part of the discontent of many young people with the culture and politics of fascism. The "discovery of race" constituted a very important cultural fact for these young people, offering them a *key* finally to "understanding" the reason for the inadequacy of fascist culture up to that moment and enabling them to react to it in the name of new *values*.[47]

To understand how anti-Semitism was able to attract many young fascists who were critical of fascist culture and politics, we must briefly examine its nature here. Unlike the Nazi anti-Semitism he was often accused of copying, Mussolini's doctrine did not rest upon a pseudo-biological racism. Indeed, he continued to regard Nazi racial doctrine as unmitigated nonsense. As late as 1940 we find him telling his official biographer that there was no such thing as an "Italian race," and that the Italian spiritual climate acted to dissipate the purity of any race which might move to the peninsula. "All races passed through the convoluted passages of the Italian distillery," he observed, but "none camped long on our piazzas."[48]

The distinction between Italian and Jew was not a biological one in the *Weltanschauung* of Italian anti-Semitism, but rather a spiritual contrast. For Mussolini there were various spiritual types in the world, and he believed that at certain dramatic moments in history it was possible to speak of "races" becoming co-extensive with "nations." Such was the case with fascist Italy, where the genius of the Italian race (a spiritual "type") had made it possible to begin the construction of the Fascist State. Yet within that State were some recalcitrant elements, which did not share in the qualities of the "race," which did not adapt to the new spiritual climate of the period, and which insisted on clinging to the values and goals of an earlier, corrupt epoch. The purpose of the anti-Semitic policies, as viewed by the Duce, was to retrain these elements, to Italianize and "fascisticize" them, and finally to reintegrate them back into fascist society.[49] When this reintegration was achieved, the Italian "race" and the Fascist State would be co-extensive, both geographically and spiritually.

It is important to stress the differences between the Nazi and the fascist conception of human nature which are reflected in the different versions of racism in the two countries. In an article on race which Mussolini considered very important, Mario Missiroli argued that ". . . the highest spiritual values are a conquest of conscience, the consequence of effort and perpetual choice and, as such, are not determined by natural fact. . . ."[50] This is clearly a dynamic theory of human nature, quite different from the Nazi concept, which was ineluctably tied to a changeless racial principle. The fascists insisted upon their ability to change the human spirit.

Mussolini's own language leaves little doubt about the "spiritual" nature of his racist thinking. Above all, the dictator's hatred was aimed at those Italians who did not feel themselves as such, who did not sense their "race." The goal of his racial policies was the transformation of the Italian people from "a race of slaves" to "a race of masters."[51] He even went so far at one point as to advocate his discriminatory policies on the grounds that they would intensify foreign antagonism toward Italy, and thus make all Italians aware of their uniqueness in the world.

In keeping with this spiritual concept of race, Italian anti-Semitic policy was aimed at the transformation of people rather than at their destruction. Mussolini himself termed this a policy of "discrimination," not "persecution."[52] Indeed, from his own warped point of view, Mussolini saw himself embarking upon a program of disciplining Italians, not launching a mass persecution. He believed that he could "Italianize" the Jews in short order: "The patriotic Jew loses the polemic characteristics of the race . . . I have Aryanized these men of great spirit. . . . It will be a question of a generation. Mixed marriages are slowly eliminating the Jewish characteristics."[53]

We can now appreciate the appeal of Italian racism to some of the more articulate and critical elements of Italian youth. In particular, the notion that the spiritual failings of the Italian people explained the failure of fascism to achieve a genuine revolution was one which many young fascist intellectuals had embraced, albeit without the "racist" framework. While the racist doctrines were anathema to many who viewed them as foreign to Italian tradition, to others Mussolini's racism offered an explanation for the prior failure of fascist culture and organization. For these, embracing racism reinforced what was, after all, already established within the framework of the doctrines of universal fascism: the belief that the successful development of the Fascist Revolution awaited the emergence of a new spiritual type. Furthermore, the racist "explanation" of fascist failures, namely, the existence of spiritually limited people rather than dynamic and creative fascists, fitted well with many of the criticisms which young fascists had directed at their elders. Many young fascists could view racism as an idea which only young people could embrace, an idea which did not find support in the ranks of the older generations because they were not ready for such a "revolutionary" step. This is the sort of rationale which De Felice has in mind when he speaks of racism as embodying a reaction to fascist culture in the name of "new values."

We can see the theme of "new values" and the "new man" at work in those areas of fascist culture produced by the supporters of racism. It is clearly elaborated in one of the last major journalistic attempts to promulgate the doctrine of universal fascism, a special issue of *Universalità Fascista* brought out in October, 1937, which reprinted a series of speeches that had been delivered at the Foreign Student Center in Rome on the theme "The Universality of Fascism."

Anti-Semitism was not mentioned explicitly in any of the lectures, yet many of the speakers referred to it indirectly.[54] The year 1937 was, after all, that in which the regime had conducted the first major press campaign on behalf of the new policies. Further, a new and strident emphasis on anti-communism had entered the pages of *Universalità Fascista*. Whereas earlier in the thirties fascism had been contrasted with liberalism, communism, and National Socialism, the major contrast in 1937 was with communism. Indeed, in some articles anti-communism had become the "universal" content of fascism itself: "It is here that fascism assumes universal value, because it undertakes as its task the struggle to save the values of the spirit against the monstrosity of a system which makes man a piece of an enormous social machine...."[55]

The conception which permeated all the speeches of 1937 was that of the new fascist man, a man who had "transcended" the old problems of liberal society. "When fascism speaks ... of educating the race, of family, of health, of educating labor ... it is not inspired by purely material interests. ... but by a higher concept...."[56]

The main thrust of these arguments was aptly summarized by Fantini. He raised the question, if the essence of fascism had to be distilled into a single word, what word would it be? And his answer was "Heroism."[57] Chanting, "Better to live one day as a lion than a hundred years as a sheep," Fantini turned to a lengthy discourse on the meaning of heroism:

> Behold, here ... the profound content of the Revolution, which is above all a new idea of life, a total and integral interpretation of the world. Man is no longer considered ... as a creature

subject to nature; life is not viewed as a burden which is born resignedly; but he is . . . a fighter, a soldier, who every day must conquer glory. . . .

Fascist Italy today is itself the concrete embodiment of heroism. Instead of the hero-man our times see the hero-nation. And the new heroism projects itself no longer on the internal life of the nation, but on the life of all nations, as something higher, noble, sublime.

. . . The struggle which the Italian people, fascist people, fight is the revelation of a state of mind which transforms men, things, and the spirit into a splendid reality. . . .[58]

This is a far cry from the earlier prophets of universal fascism, who had foreseen the creation of Dante's Empire on the basis of Italian civilization rather than on military virtues. Further, Fantini's definition of an Italian hero-nation which would embody the military virtues contains all the essential elements of Italian racism. All that is necessary to complete the doctrine is to cast the Jew as antithesis of the hero.

So we see that the "new man," who in the early thirties had been described as an iconoclast, an enemy of the fascist hierarchy, and an innovator on a worldwide scale, has been transformed into a soldier in the ranks. Further, while the appeal was still aimed at young people, much of the rhetoric associated with the cult of Youth had vanished from the *universalfascismo* propaganda.

So, many young fascist intellectuals were captured by the regime's anti-Semitic programs in the late thirties and forties. Indeed, one of the bitter ironies of the fascist period is the degree to which the youth finally found themselves isolated by the development of fascism, and the consequent turn by some to the racist "answer" offered by the regime.

To say this, however, is to identify one of the very few groups which supported fascist anti-Semitism; and even within the ranks of fascist youth, there were very many who could not accept the foreign doctrine of racism, so that the passage of the laws of 1938 marked the end of their participation in the fascist enterprise. Many of the young intellectuals who had previously supported the regime turned to an active, anti-fascist opposition to Mussolini himself. Members of the "fascist generation" who had believed that fascism could become a truly viable means of social transformation were catalyzed into open revolt by the adoption of the racial measures. Deeply disturbed by fascism's failure to produce any meaningful changes in Italian society, by its inability to generate a culture worthy of Italian tradition, and by its increasing closeness to the Nazis, many young intellectuals joined with those who had already turned on Mussolini. They did so for a variety of reasons, but above all because the changes in fascism in this period had stripped from them the "conditional liberty" they had enjoyed earlier, and because they were forced to submit to a racist policy and a German alliance which they found odious.[59]

This opposition took many forms in the late thirties and early forties, and an investigation of such activities would take us far afield. But it must be mentioned that the resistance to fascism on the part of youth took, generally speaking, two basic forms. The first was the path of clear and open revolt against the regime itself. This was the one taken by Ruggero Zangrandi and his companions in his "long journey across fascism."[60] The second was that taken by Gastone Silvano Spinetti, of remaining within fascist society while continuing to try to transform it, to make it into something worthwhile. These were the young people who continued to call themselves "fascists" even while they agitated against the regime and against its policies. Spinetti has described them thus:

> [They were] young people who were not true anti-Fascists, because in order to profess their own ideas freely they called themselves "Mussolinians," but in reality they practiced a good

and beautiful anti-fascism, perhaps more productive in Italy than that practiced from outside by the *émigrés*, criticizing the hierarchs, the institutions, and even the principles proclaimed by the "fascist doctrine."[61]

These were among the young people who had agitated so forcefully for universal fascism, and who were, as Spinetti observes, *in nuce* liberals, socialists, Catholics, and Communists, but who all called themselves "fascists."[62] Having developed many critical ideas during the course of their lives in the *Ventennio*, they maintained their position of reformist agitation throughout the Axis period. When the war ended they returned to Italian politics as liberals, Christian Democrats, socialists, and Communists, and the change of political labels did not necessarily represent a profound change in attitude. The very failure of fascism genuinely to indoctrinate and integrate young intellectuals into the fabric of the regime produced a generation that possessed considerable independence, an independence they would demonstrate after the fall of fascism when many of them participated in the creation of the Italian Republic.

CONCLUSION:

The Incomplete Revolution

◢◣ In 1926 William Bolitho, the brilliant American reporter for the New York *World*, returned to his native Italy to study fascism. After a penetrating analysis of many of the accomplishments and defects of Mussolini and his allies, Bolitho concluded that "Fascism is a social disease, a fever of the body politic, brought on by disorganized industry and general depression. There is no more a doctrine of Fascism than a doctrine of smallpox."[1]

This is one of the earliest expressions of what was to become a widespread conviction: that Italian fascism was ideologically barren, and had to be understood in terms of special interest groups, reaction to depression and war, and the like. Although these views neither originated with nor were held solely by left-wing analysts, the classic example of such an evaluation of fascism was adopted by the Comintern when it defined fascism as the last, desperate attempt by the capitalist bourgeoisie to defend bourgeois society against its own internal contradictions.[2] Such ideas as emerged from this reactionary form of government were to be viewed as simple rationalizations for the need to seize power and to defend the State against its class enemies of the proletariat.

This view of fascism's lack of a coherent intellectual base was also held by many fascists, especially in the early twenties. As late as 1923 Dino Grandi, one of the heroes of the March on Rome, could complain of fascism's lack of a theoretical framework, and Mussolini himself often boasted of its pragmatic nature, its ability to alter its stance as events recommended change. Finally, the historian of the fascist period, Luigi Salvatorelli, advocated the same position:

> [The Italian people] . . . hated the spirit of fascism itself. . . . Fascist theories did not go beyond the chewed-over ideas of the nationalists, which the philosopher of the regime, Gentile, tried in vain to endow with the aspect of politico-moral thought. . . . The Italian people, having been outside political life for centuries, tended to become so again after the interlude of the *Risorgimento* and post-*Risorgimento*, thanks to fascism. . . .[3]

Thus, a tradition developed which treated Italian fascism as a transitory political phenomenon, more or less foisted off on the Italian people by Mussolini, the supreme demagogue. Fascism was seen as an extension of the personality of the Duce rather than as a viable political movement in its own right, and consequently the history of fascism and the biography of Mussolini were viewed as more or less co-extensive. Herman Finer, in his classic study, *Mussolini's Italy*, argued that the fascist period had been an extension of Mussolini's character ("He had been able to grip the Italian people in that character from October, 1922 . . . until the Allies had begun to set the Italian people free . . . in the late fall of 1942").[4] With the death of Mussolini, the fascist period came to an end and the more "natural" impulses of the Italian people emerged. This was the view of Croce for many years, when he considered fascism to have been an "accident" of Italian history. Again, Finer summed up this view when he wrote:

> Soon after the invasion, the indigenous passion of the Italians for political liberty and human decency surged out openly. . . . Above all, they began to clear away the miasma of truculent

braggadocio and romantic impotence which had inspired fascism and degraded the nation. . . .[5]

Fascism, then, has traditionally been viewed as the imposition of a regime of counterrevolutionaries and opportunists upon the Italian people. Yet, there is a growing body of information which exposes several weaknesses in this view. In the first place, when fascism came to power it was hardly a reactionary movement. All sorts of socialists, syndicalists, and anarcho-syndicalists had enlisted in Mussolini's ranks, and the tendency of early fascism seemed to many to be towards the Left rather than towards the imposition of a "white terror." To be sure, fascism evolved in the direction of a conservative regime favoring the vested interests of Italian society, but only a small number of very perceptive observers could see such a regime emerging from the fascist movement, and as late as the early thirties such a man as Giuseppe Bottai still thought it possible to "revolutionize" fascism.

Furthermore, as fascism developed, it acquired increasing support from the Italian people, and especially during the period 1925–30, Mussolini developed a *national* base quite independent of any narrowly class-based support. It is the emergence of fascism as a popular national phenomenon which requires explanation, and that explanation cannot be found by investigating fascism's undoubted support of particular interests in Italy. This is the point made recently by Renzo De Felice in his monumental biography of Mussolini, when he said that while fascism undoubtedly had class-bound characteristics, these do not explain its success nor its widespread appeal among all levels of the Italian populace.[6]

We have tried to analyze fascism's appeal among educated and intelligent Italians during a portion of the fascist *Ventennio*. In so doing, we have tried to consider a part of fascist rhetoric which has received very little attention by scholars, namely, the attempt to transform fascism from a national to an international movement in the late twenties and early thirties. We raised the question of the appeal of fascism to people beyond the boundaries of Italy, as well as to elements within the peninsula. On the basis of this examination, it would seem that the traditional accounts of fascist ideology should be reconsidered.

Few people were more acutely aware of the shortcomings of fascist theory and practice than the educated young fascists who were raised after the March on Rome of October, 1922. These young Italians, who constituted a "fascist generation," genuinely wanted to transform fascism into a phenomenon which could achieve a thorough change in Italian society, and so provide the basis for restructuring all Western societies. If this grandiose prospect seems somewhat exaggerated to us, it did not to many intellectuals and statesmen, fascist and nonfascist alike, in the turbulent thirties in Europe. Many took the possibility very seriously indeed, as the meeting of representatives from fascist movements in thirteen different European countries in 1934 shows quite clearly. It would seem, then, that Italian fascism had sufficient appeal to draw together the representatives of diverse European fascist movements.

Indeed, to say that fascism had little in the way of a coherent ideology is both to miss the point of its appeal and to grossly overstate the merits of intellectual consistency when assessing the attractiveness of political doctrines. In the first place, fascism in Italy emerged in response to a domestic crisis which many believed to have threatened the very existence of Italian society. Fascism thus had originally claimed to be a therapy for a body politic on the verge of extinction. Mussolini had not claimed doctrinal coherence at first, and the fact that fascism could appeal to a body of supporters ranging from the Nationalist Right to the anarcho-syndicalist Left demonstrated both the personal appeal of Mussolini himself and the confidence of large sectors of the Italian public that he and the men around him were capable of solving Italy's problems. Secondly, the existence of various versions of fascism, or, as we have termed it earlier, of several fascisms in the late twenties and early thirties, enabled the regime to win the confidence of people with very diverse political views, and to avoid internal rupture of the sort often associated with more "coherent" political movements. In a sense, Mussolini's Italy represented the triumph of what Americans have called "consensus politics," that is, of a form of political behavior which seeks to accommodate the maximum number of people and ideas within the framework of the nation. Its undoubted success in the early thirties is testimony to the viability of this form of political behavior, and to Mussolini's ability to convince his public that he was capable of supporting various elements within Italian society.

Thus, far from weakening the popular appeal of his regime, the very lack of any codified ideology lent fascism considerable political strength. The ability of diverse elements of Italian society to make of fascism what they wanted enabled Mussolini to deal with various threats to his own power and prestige in a way that would have been impossible in a more rigid ideological situation.

Yet it would be erroneous to treat fascism solely in terms of traditional political models, for it came to represent a revolutionary approach to Western society for many, especially young people. These young fascists believed themselves to be on the verge of a total reconstitution of their own country, and, ultimately, the entire Western world. Camillo Pellizzi has nicely characterized this as the concept of the Fascist State as a "dynamo," a generator of energy and creativity, which would liberate men from the conditions of alienation and class warfare that typified the liberal societies of the nineteenth century, and open the Fascist Era.[7] It was to be the era of youthful genius and creativity, and the most common metaphor which fascists used to contrast their own concept of the world with that of the preceding generations was the Mazzinian dichotomy of "young Italy" against "old Europe." It was this notion which lay at the heart of the attempt to create a Fascist International, and which enabled Italian fascists to claim that they were the harbingers of a new European epoch.

What was this new epoch to be? Above all, a period when society was restructured so as to remove class conflict, and where human abilities were able to develop to the fullest. Therefore, fascist writers tended to describe their future society in human terms, rather than in economic or social concepts. In accordance with Mussolini's oft-quoted dictum, "Economic man does not exist," Italian fascists looked to a period where genuine human emotions would be free to develop spontaneously. They believed that in the fascist society of the future, a new kind of mentality would develop, and that the possessors of this new mentality would restructure society in accordance with their own enhanced knowledge and sensitivity. The new society, then, could not be created by those who had been tied to outmoded conceptions of the world, but could only be brought about by those who were unfettered by previous models. So the "new fascist man" had to be found among the young, who had been raised in the heady atmosphere of fascist innovation.

It would be a considerable overstatement to call Italian fascism a youth movement, yet for a certain limited period in the late twenties and early thirties much of the energy of fascist leaders was devoted to the question of Youth and the role it would play in the Europe of the future. We have seen that this concept played a pivotal role in the emergence of the notion of universal fascism, and that the idea of a young fascism played a major part in the debates among fascist leaders at Montreux in 1934. Many scholars have dealt with the idea of the new fascist man, both in Italian and other versions of fascism, and it is significant that every fascist movement seems to have embraced this concept. The idea was a very fluid one, however, and during the history of Italian fascism, at least, the identification of the "new man" with a particular group of Italians underwent change. At first the new mentality was identified with the generation which had served Italy in the trenches of the Great War, with that "Mussolinian generation" to which the early squadrist leaders and the participants in the March on Rome belonged. But as time passed and a new generation came of age, the notion of the "new man" was used to criticize the failure of the Mussolinian generation to effect a revolutionary transformation of Italy.

This last point has occupied much of our attention in the preceding pages, and needs some comment here, for while certain scholars have recognized the centrality of the ideas of Youth and the "new man," few have noticed their connection with a serious opposition to the Fascist Regime from within the body of fascism itself. For one of our major themes has been the degree to which young fascists were alienated from the Fascist Regime in Italy, and how deeply they felt the failure of Mussolini and his generation to achieve the transformation of Italian society which had been anticipated so keenly.

Many of those who developed universal fascism did so in an attempt to change fascism itself, and the movement must consequently be considered, at least in part, a protest movement within fascism. Typically enough, that protest was cast in the moral and emotional tones which have so often been identified with the essence of fascism itself, for the young Italian critics of Mussolini's Italy felt themselves to be true fascists of the sort George L. Mosse has described as those who believed "that the creative individual, because of his attitude of mind, would solve the concrete problems which confronted the nation."[8]

Mosse was speaking of fascist intellectuals who embraced fascism in an opposition to the sterility and barrenness of the twentieth-century world. The same can be said of the young fascists and their older leaders and supporters who attempted to form a Fascist International.

This style of criticism of fascism from within demonstrates again that the very fluidity of the doctrine made it possible for the regime to accommodate itself to various impulses within Italy. It was possible for critics to attack its failures without having to break with fascism itself. And it is perhaps ironic that fascism's critics used doctrines which have been considered exquisitely "fascist" to criticize the failures of Mussolini. Yet this helps to demonstrate not only the lack of firm doctrinal guidelines in fascist Italy, but also the good faith of the critics. They were not, for the most part, genuine anti-fascists, but simply disgruntled believers in fascism.

The attempt to develop a doctrine of universal fascism suggests also that there were impulses within the fabric of Italian fascist society which tended to look beyond the boundaries of Italy in defining their world-view. Thus, while fascism has traditionally been dealt with in terms of hyper-nationalism, we have seen that it had a trans-national appeal as well, and the attempt to establish a Fascist International at Montreux in 1934 needs to be taken with some seriousness despite its paucity of concrete results. In the first place, the mere fact that the regime authorized such a meeting demonstrates the change which had taken place in the evaluation of fascism by Mussolini and the other hierarchs in Rome since the days when the Duce's slogan, "Fascism is not merchandise for export," had been common coin. This transformation of fascist doctrine points to the success with which those critics of the regime had voiced their own conception of the role of fascism in the world, and also to Mussolini's receptivity to such a change. Secondly, Mussolini's willingness to lend the prestige of his government to the Montreux meeting under the auspices of the CAUR reflects his own growing excitement over the prospects of expanding Italian influence over European affairs in the middle thirties. The declarations of admiration for Italian fascism which had come from all over Europe at the Volta Congress were a representative cross-sample of a growing body of support for the Italian experiment. Thirdly, the broad representation at Montreux points to the ability of fascism to recruit enthusiastic support from countries with diverse national traditions and circumstances, and suggests at least the possibility that fascism truly was a European phenomenon, that, in the words of Ernst Nolte, the period between the two world wars must be considered "the fascist epoch."[9]

Yet the events at Montreux which we have examined suggest that Nolte's thesis requires substantial modification. There was consensus, to be sure, at Montreux, on the desire for the spread of fascism, and for the emergence of "young forces" for change and regeneration throughout the old continent. But there was a disturbing conflict of opinion at Montreux which no amount of enthusiasm for youth could cover over, and that conflict pointed to a profound cleavage within the ranks of those who called themselves "fascist." The dispute over the "Jewish question" at Montreux caused (as we have seen) considerable consternation not only among the delegates to the Congress, but also among fascist leaders in Rome, for it showed that the issue of racism went very deeply indeed into the structure of European fascism. In the end, it proved to be of fatal importance, for those who were dedicated to removing the Jews from European society could not, in the last analysis, successfully ally themselves with an Italy which not only seemed unaware of the "Jewish question" but which became a haven for European Jewish refugees in the years after 1933.

The debate at Montreux anticipated the inner tensions of the Axis Pact; and just as the racist issue was unresolvable on an international scale in 1934, it would remain so in the late thirties and early forties. The "brutal friendship" between Hitler and Mussolini remained a personal alliance, and the strongly negative domestic reaction which it provoked in Italy is testimony to the seriousness of the conflict already seen at Montreux. Indeed, Mussolini's adoption of a doctrine which had been anathema to many of his most fervent supporters drastically weakened his position. The introduction of anti-Semitism by the Italian regime in 1938 alienated fascism from the majority of Italians, just as they had opposed German anti-Semitism earlier in the decade.

It does not seem unreasonable to claim, therefore, that European fascist movements ought to be dealt with in two main categories: those that advocated racism and those that did not. This deep division within the ranks of European fascists has frequently been treated as if it were a mere question of policy, something which represented a pragmatic decision for each fascist movement, based on nearness to Nazi Germany, sources of foreign financial support, or other similar considerations. Yet the Montreux Congress revealed differences which were to remain serious ones throughout the thirties and the Second World War; those movements which raised the specter of racism in Switzerland in 1934 remained committed to that doctrine.

This profound division has been termed a difference between western and central European fascism by George L. Mosse:

> The open-endedness of much of European fascism, its ideological fluidity under authoritarian leadership, strengthened its attraction. German National Socialism must be listed as an exception here. . . . In the West, at any rate, the fascist movements, and the intellectuals who were involved, looked to Italy rather than central Europe for inspiration. It is, therefore, dangerous to extend the ideological foundations of the German fascist experience to that of other countries.[10]

It would seem that this statement is not strong enough for those fascists we have dealt with, both in Italy and abroad, who were attracted to the ideal of a Fascist International but did not embrace the racist doctrine. What is important here is the violent hatred, even loathing, of Hitler's racism by many Italians and other fascists who looked for the "new man" and the youthful transformation of the continent. This highly emotional reaction, which flooded the pages of those journals dedicated to the doctrine of universal fascism, would manifest itself in an outright break with fascism itself when Mussolini adopted the foreign ideology of anti-Semitism in the late thirties.

To echo for a moment the view of many of the young fascists dealt with here, the period which began in 1938 represented a betrayal of fascism by the hierarchs of the Italian State. At that moment all those who had truly believed in the unique genius of each national fascism revolted against the imposition of a foreign tradition and an alien ideology upon the Italian people. It was at that point that many Italians could clearly see that all hope for a genuine transformation of Italy along the lines advocated by fascist theorists had to be abandoned under Mussolini's regime. Thus one might be tempted to say that Mussolini was finally overthrown by those who had taken him most seriously before 1938, and who were profoundly alienated by his adoption of the Nazi credo. Many of those who forced Mussolini out of office in 1943 had been his closest collaborators, and the later trials at Verona, when Mussolini purged many of his former friends (including Ciano, his son-in-law), lend further substance to this claim.

Yet to say this would be to ignore two small but crucial groups in the history of the fascist *Ventennio*: the members of the Resistance, and those like Giuseppe Bottai who continued to agitate for changes within fascism at the same time as they adopted the doctrines of anti-Semitism. Bottai was in the front ranks of the *universalfascismo* movement, and was a highly inspirational figure for those young fascists who recognized the failures of the regime while still retaining a commitment to the creation of a fascist utopia. This adoption of anti-Semitism suggests that racism, while alien to Italian tradition, was not necessarily unacceptable to certain elements within fascism.

In his study of the Italian Jews under fascism, Renzo De Felice argued that only two groups within Italian society provided any substantial support for the anti-Semitic policies of Mussolini: youth and those engaged in the creation of a "fascist culture." De Felice further suggested that the explanation for this behavior was to be found in the bankruptcy of Italian culture under fascism, and the terrible tension in the ranks of youth. This interpretation would seem to be borne out by our investigation of universal fascism. For many young fascists who had committed their passions and energies to the expansion of fascism and the creation of a viable ideology for that expansion, the collapse of the movement for a Fascist International and the alliance with Hitler represented a cultural shock of great magnitude. To such people, anti-Semitism offered a possible rationalization for the failures of fascist society, and a target on which they could respectably vent their anger. As suggested earlier, many broke with the regime when the anti-Semitic legislation was promulgated; others, unable to bring themselves to the point of turning against their own government, turned against the "enemy within," the Jews.

Yet it remains true that Italian anti-Semitism was marginal at best. The great majority of Italians rejected the racial doctrines, and the distinction which we have suggested between Nazism and fascism was confirmed by the reaction of Italian fascists to the 1938 legislation.

Finally, our investigation into the doctrines of universal fascism confirms the view held by many scholars of Italian fascism, that the regime never succeeded in becoming truly "totalitarian." The dramatic failure of Mussolini's Italy to enlist the full and unquestioned support of its youth, and successfully to bring the schools and intellectuals under complete control makes it impossible to claim that the Fascist Regime held sway over the hearts and minds of the majority of educated Italians. Mussolini's own personal popularity was undoubtedly very strong indeed, but there continued to be a substantial amount of criticism and opposition to many of the dictator's ideas and programs. The significant number of independent-minded young people during the *Ventennio*, from Mussolini's son on down, indicates that the Italian tradition of independence and cynical distrust of authority was not subjugated totally by fascism, even though many of the hierarchs tried to institute rigid control over the populace. A most striking failure of fascism was its inability to provide for the creation of a new ruling class, for the education and assimilation of a new élite in Italian society, committed to the further development and institutionalization of the Fascist State. This new élite was to have come from fascist youth, yet many of the best elements of fascist youth were highly critical of the regime.

This theme, which we have seen repeatedly during the late twenties and early thirties, constitutes the basic insight of a moving and fundamental work on Italian fascism, *Una Rivoluzione Mancata (The Incomplete Revolution,* 1949) by Camillo Pellizzi. For Pellizzi, whose sympathies toward fascism and toward the attempt to create a Fascist International have been amply demonstrated in earlier chapters, the supreme irony of the *Ventennio* was that the cries which the fascists had directed against the leaders of the post-*Risorgimento* came to be leveled at the fascist hierarchs themselves during the Second World War. The mentality which Pellizzi evoked in his analysis of fascism might well serve us as an excellent summary of the attitudes and ideas we have been concerned with:

[Mussolini's generation] tended to hypostasize in its own mind an ideal Italy, made up of grand traditions, great figures, and high sentiments, imagining this to be the true and valid Italy, on which it believed or judged that the little men of politics and public administration flowed like a swarm of repugnant or damnable parasites.[11]

The task of fascism was to rescue the true Italy from the voracious parasites which were draining its energies and life forces. And for a while, Pellizzi claimed, it seemed that fascism was on the verge of liberating those energies and forces. The frustration of the "fascist generation" was that this transformation of Italy seemed to be so near, yet was not accomplished:

. . . there was . . . the first half of a true and genuine social revolution; but there was not then the clarity, the will, the courage, or the possibility of proceeding to the second part. The Corporate Order was at once a theoretical and a practical compromise, halfway between the first and second half of this "revolution." In the sphere of programme, the revolution was already implicit in the postulates of that Order; but it never became totally explicit, and never entered into the realm of fact.[12]

This was the frustrating and tantalizing condition in which young fascists lived during the reign of Mussolini, and the zeal with which they pursued the fulfillment of the incomplete revolution only added to the frustration of those Italians who sought to actualize the theories of universal fascism.

Notes

Bibliography

Index

A Note on the Use of Sources

⋀⋀⋀ The sources on Italian fascism are simultaneously inadequate and overwhelming. On the one hand, such vital information as the finances of various offices during the *Ventennio* are not yet accessible; on the other, we are inundated by thousands of volumes on fascist theory and propaganda. In addition, the archival material that is available is often very delicate and suggestive, and it is not always possible to cite archival sources when they refer to living persons. With this in mind, an attempt has been made to refer to archival material where possible; when not possible, reference has been made to the closest reliable secondary source. In the case of quotations from secondary sources, every attempt has been made to check their accuracy. All translations are my own.

Introduction

1. Cf. Denis Mack Smith, *Italy; A Modern History* (Ann Arbor, Mich., 1959), 399.
2. Cf. Ernst Nolte, *Three Faces of Fascism* (New York, 1966); Stuart Woolf's Introduction to the volume edited by him, *European Fascism* (London, 1968); George L. Mosse, "Fascism and the Intellectuals," in Stuart Woolf, ed., *The Nature of Fascism* (London, 1969).
3. Mack Smith, *op. cit.*, 411.
4. Cf. Gastone Silvano Spinetti, *La Difesa di una generazione* (Rome, 1949), and Ruggero Zangrandi, *Il lungo viaggio attraverso il fascismo* (Milan, 1962).
5. Cf. H. S. Harris, *The Social Philosophy of Giovanni Gentile* (Urbana, Ill., and London, 1966), 155–167.
6. Fritz Stern, *The Politics of Cultural Despair* (Berkeley and Los Angeles, Calif., 1961).
7. John Thayer, *Italy and the Great War* (Madison, Wis., 1964).
8. Cf. U. Foscanelli, *D'Annunzio e il fascismo* (Milan, 1923).
9. Nolte, *op. cit.*, 221.
10. Or this is the interpretation one gains from Mack Smith's account of fascism in *op. cit.*, 390–405.
11. Federico Chabod, *L'Italia Contemporanea (1918–1948)* (Turin, 1968), 88.

Chapter One: *Fascism and Youth*

1. Cf., for example, Foscanelli, *op. cit.*, esp. Ch. 4.
2. The literature on futurism is substantial. The most complete original source is F. T. Marinetti, *Teoria e invenzione futurista*

(Verona, 1968). For a wider cross section, cf. Luigi Scrivo, *Sintesi del futurismo* (Rome, 1968).

3. The statement is taken from an article in the Neapolitan newspaper *Roma*, August 22, 1923. Quoted in Marinetti, *op. cit.*, 429–30.
4. This is Marinetti's famous work of 1915.
5. Quoted in Marinetti, *op. cit.*, 463.
6. *Ibid.*, 465.
7. Cf. the testimony to this effect by Massimo Rocca, *Il Primo fascismo* (Rome, 1964), esp. Chs. 4–6.
8. The entire statute can be found in Edoardo and Duilio Susmel, eds., *Opera Omnia di Benito Mussolini* (Florence, 1954–63), XVII, 345–349. Henceforth this collection will be referred to as Mussolini, *Opera Omnia*.
9. Cf. Rocca, *op. cit.*, esp. Ch. 5.
10. Cited in Alberto Aquarone, "Aspirazioni tecnocratiche del primo fascismo," in *Nord e Sud*, May, 1964.
11. Quoted in Herman Finer, *Mussolini's Italy* (New York, 1965), 428.
12. *Ibid.*, 428–429.
13. *Ibid.*, 428.
14. Archivio Centrale dello Stato (henceforth abbreviated as ACS), *Segretaria particolare del Duce, carteggio riservato (1922–1943)*, fasc. 242/R, *Riunione del Direttorio Del PNF*, sottofasc. 2.
15. *Ibid.*
16. *Ibid.*
17. ACS, *Segr. part. del Duce, cart. ris. (1922–1943)*, fasc. 242/R, *Starace*, sottofasc. 1.
18. Cf. Carlo Ludovico Ragghianti, "Il fascismo e la cultura," in L. Arbizzani and A. Caltabiano, eds., *Storia dell'antifascismo Italiano* (Rome, 1964), I, esp. 105–106.
19. Quoted in Ottavio Dinale, *Quarant'anni di colloqui con lui* (Milan, 1953), 181.
20. Cf., for example, Giorgio Luti, *Cronache letterarie tra le due guerre 1920/1940* (Bari, 1966).
21. This is one of the major themes of G. S. Spinetti, *op. cit.*
22. Cf. Zangrandi, *op. cit.*, 141–159.
23. Quoted in Renzo De Felice, *Fascismo e Partiti Politici Italiani* (Bologna, 1966), 12.

24. *Popolo d'Italia*, August 24, 1928.
25. *Ibid.*, April 26, 1929.
26. *Ibid.*
27. *Ibid.*, May 31, 1929.
28. *Ibid.*, October 28, 1930.
29. *Ibid.*, November 11, 1930.
30. *Ibid.*, October 28, 1930.
31. Cf. G. S. Spinetti, ed., *Mistica Fascista nel pensiero di Arnaldo Mussolini* (Milan, 1936), x.
32. *Ibid.*
33. *Ibid.*, 206–207.
34. *Ibid.*, 217–218.
35. Information on the organization and operation of the School is very difficult to locate. One of the most useful sources is the files of the *Ministero della cultura popolare* (henceforth abbreviated *Minculpop*). Cf. ACS, *Minculpop*, Busta 84, fasc. 1, *Atti vari della Scuola di Mistica Fascista Sandro Italico Mussolini*.
36. *Ibid.*
37. Mussolini, *Opera Omnia*, XXV, 147.

Chapter Two: *Youth and Universal Fascism*

1. The literature on Bottai is voluminous. The most compact summary of his life is in Roberto Bartolozzi and Riccardo Del Giudice, eds., *Scritti di Giuseppe Bottai* (Rome, 1965), 409–411. This volume is also extremely useful for a purview of Bottai's intellectual history.
2. *Critica Fascista*, January 1, 1928.
3. *Ibid.*
4. *Ibid.*, June 15, 1930.
5. *Ibid.*
6. *Ibid.*
7. *Ibid.*, January 1, 1930.
8. *Ibid.*, February 1, 1930.
9. *Ibid.*
10. *Ibid.*
11. *Ibid.*
12. Cf. Giovanni Fioridi Della Lena, "Università Fascismo," in *Critica Fascista*, August 1, 1930.
13. *Critica Fascista*, October 15, 1930.

14. *Ibid.*
15. *Ibid.*, December 15, 1930.
16. *Ibid.*
17. *Ibid.*, January 15, 1933.
18. *Ibid.*
19. *Ibid.*, January 1, 1930.
20. *Ibid.*
21. *Ibid.*, March 1, 1933.
22. *Ibid.*
23. *Ibid.*
24. *Ibid.*, April 15, 1933.
25. *Ibid.*
26. A description of the activities of the "Novismo" group can be found in Zangrandi, *op. cit.*, 33–42.
27. "Una circolare del Movimento Novista Italiano," September, 1933, reproduced in Zangrandi, *op. cit.*, 453–455.
28. Enzo Santarelli, *Storia del movimento e del regime fascista* (Rome, 1967), II, 74–75.
29. G. S. Spinetti, *Vent'anni dopo ricominciare da zero* (Rome, 1964), 65.
30. *La Sapienza*, January, 1933.
31. *Ibid.*
32. Cf. *La Sapienza* for May and June–July, 1933.
33. *Ibid.*, May, 1933.
34. *Ibid.*
35. *Ibid.*, April, 1933.
36. G. S. Spinetti, *Fascismo Universale* (Rome, 1934), 6.
37. *Ibid.*, 25.
38. *Ibid.*, 27–28.
39. *La Sapienza*, February, 1933.
40. *Ibid.*, January, 1933.
41. The files of Mussolini's private secretary are full of such references. Cf. ACS, *Segr. part. del Duce, cart. ris. (1922–1943)*, Busta 1, Fasc. 7/R, *Giovanni Gentile*, sottofasc. 6, *Rilievi al suo carico*.
42. *Ibid.*
43. *Ibid.*
44. *Ibid.*
45. *Ibid.*

46. The report is dated February 21, 1940. ACS, *Minculpop*, Busta 84, fasc. 1, *Atti vari della Scuola di Mistica Fascista Sandro Italico Mussolini*.
47. *Ibid.*
48. G. S. Spinetti, *L'Europa verso la Rivoluzione* (Rome, 1936), 12.
49. *Ibid.*, 58.
50. G. S. Spinetti, *Fascismo e Libertà* (Padua, 1941), ix.
51. *Ibid.*, 4.
52. *Ibid.*, x.
53. *Ibid.*, 12.
54. Cf. Zangrandi, *op. cit.*, 141–159. Also his "I giovani e il fascismo," in *Fascismo e antifascismo (1918–1936)* (Milan, 1962), I, 209–216.
55. G. S. Spinetti, *Vent'anni dopo.*, *op. cit.*, 79.
56. *Ibid.*, 80.
57. *L'Universale*, January, 1931.
58. *Ibid.*
59. *Ibid.*
60. *Ibid.*
61. *Ibid.*
62. *Ibid.*
63. One claim that the Fascist Revolution represented the fourth time Italy saved the world is in *Gerarchia*, October, 1932.
64. *L'Universale*, January, 1931.
65. *Ibid.*
66. *Ibid.*
67. *Ibid.*
68. *Il Saggiatore*, April, 1930.
69. *Ibid.*
70. *Ibid.*
71. Gioacchino Volpe, *The History of the Fascist Movement* (Rome, 1936), 161.
72. Cf. George L. Mosse, "The Genesis of Fascism," in G. L. Mosse and W. Laqueur, eds., *International Fascism 1920–1945* (New York, 1966), 18–21.
73. Benito Mussolini, *Scritti e Discorsi*, ed. V. Piccoli (Rome, 1934), VII, 230.
74. *Ibid.*

Chapter Three: *Towards the International*

1. Cf. Adrian Lyttelton, "Fascism in Italy: The Second Wave," in Mosse and Laqueur, eds., *op. cit.*, 75–100, for an example of the sort of pressure Mussolini was subject to.
2. Cf. Luigi Salvatorelli and Giovanni Mira, *Storia d'Italia nel periodo fascista* (Turin, 1961), 329–360.
3. Cf. Renzo De Felice, *Mussolini il fascista. II: L'organizzazione dello Stato fascista* (Turin, 1968), 139–221, and Alberto Aquarone, *L'organizzazione dello Stato totalitario* (Turin, 1965), Chs. 4 and 5.
4. Cf. De Felice, *Mussolini il fascista, op. cit.*, 222–297.
5. *Ibid.*
6. For Rossoni's ideas on syndicalism, cf. his "Gli svillupi del sindacalismo fascista," in *Il Regime Fascista*, January 17–18, 1926.
7. De Felice, *op. cit.*, 335–340.
8. Cf. Aquarone, *op. cit.*, 293–300.
9. This is the testimony of the chief of the Secret Police. Cf. Guido Leto, *OVRA. Fascismo-antifascismo* (Bologna, 1962).
10. De Felice, *op. cit.*, 129–138.
11. *Critica Fascista*, January 1, 1929.
12. Including Finer, De Felice, Aquarone, and Salvatorelli.
13. Stefano Jacini, *Il regime fascista* (n.p., 1947), 51.
14. Cf. Carmen Haidor, *Capital and Labor under Fascism* (New York, 1930), and Giuseppe Bottai, *Esperienza corporativa* (Florence, 1934).
15. Mussolini, *Opera Omnia*, XXII, 241.
16. *Critica Fascista*, June 15, 1930.
17. Cf. De Felice, *op. cit.*, 275–296.
18. *Critica Fascista*, June 15, 1930.
19. De Felice, *op. cit.*, 359.
20. Leto, *op. cit.*
21. *L'Epoca*, February 24, 1925.
22. Cf. Giuseppe Bottai, *Vent'anni e un giorno* (Rome, 1949), 57–59.
23. *Critica Fascista*, February 15, 1933.
24. *Ibid.*
25. *Ibid.*, December 1, 1933.

26. Cf., for example, Angelo Del Boca and Mario Giovana, *I "figli del sole"* (Milan, 1965), 93–107.
27. Santarelli, *op. cit.*, II, 77.
28. *Antieuropa*, November–December, 1930.
29. *Ibid.*
30. Reproduced in Asvero Gravelli, *Verso L'Internazionale Fascista* (Rome, 1932), 32.
31. *Ibid.*, 95.
32. *Antieuropa*, September 30, 1933.
33. *Ottobre*, June 5, 1934.
34. Cf. Santarelli, *op. cit.*, II, 140–142.
35. *Ibid.* Cf. also *Ottobre*, January 15, 1933.
36. *Ottobre*, January 15, 1933.
37. Quoted in *Ottobre*, February 1, 1933.
38. Cf., for example, Gravelli's editorial in *Ottobre*, January 15, 1933.
39. Gravelli, *op. cit.*, 203–220.
40. *Ottobre*, December 1, 1933.
41. *Ibid.*, July 16, 1933.
42. *Ibid.*
43. *Ibid.*, March 1, 1933.
44. *Ibid.*, July 1, 1933.
45. Centre International d'Études sur le Fascisme ("Cinef"), *Yearbook* (Lausanne, 1928).
46. *Ibid.*, 5–7.
47. *Ibid.*, 9.
48. James Strachey Barnes, *The Universal Aspects of Fascism* (London, 1928).
49. "Cinef," *op. cit.*, 16.
50. Barnes, *op. cit.*, 25.
51. *Ibid.*, 126–127.
52. *Ibid.*, 98–99.
53. *Ibid.*, 164.
54. *Ibid.*, 167–169.
55. *Ibid.*, 59, 70.
56. *Universalità Romana*, March–April, 1932.
57. *Ibid.*
58. Cf. Ferri's remarks about Gravelli in *Universalità Romana*, May–June, 1932.

59. *Ibid.*, January, 1933.
60. *Ibid.*, November–December, 1932.
61. Zangrandi, *op. cit.*, 141–160.
62. *Universalità Fascista*, May–June, 1931.
63. Carlo Curcio, Introduction to Oddone Fantini, *Universalità del fascismo* (Naples, 1933).
64. Fantini, *op. cit.*, 27.
65. Spinetti, *op. cit.*, 33.
66. Zangrandi, *loc cit.*
67. Cf. Renzo De Felice, "Una pagina ignota dei rapporti Hitler-Mussolini," in *Corriere della Sera*, February 19, 1968.
68. Cf. Salvatorelli and Mira, *op. cit.*, 411–415.
69. Cf. Finer, *op. cit.*, 94.
70. *Universalità Romana*, II, 3–4 (1933).
71. Cf. Ludwig Jedlicka, "The Austrian Heimwehr," in Mosse and Laqueur, eds., *op. cit.*, 134–138. Also Del Boca and Giovana, *op. cit.*, 31.
72. *Ottobre*, May 1, 1934.
73. *Universalità Fascista*, November, 1936.
74. *Ottobre*, October 28, 1932.
75. *Ibid.*, February 1, 1933.
76. *Ibid.*, June 15, 1933.
77. *Ibid.*, September 1, 1933.
78. *Ibid.*, January 9, 1935.
79. *Ibid.*, March 3, 1934.
80. *Ibid.*, April 2, 1934.
81. *Ibid.*, April 12, 1934.
82. *Ibid.*, May 10, 1934.
83. Cf. Renzo De Felice, *Storia degli ebrei italiani sotto il fascismo* (Turin, 1961), 75–90, 125–134, 162–173.
84. G. Pini and D. Susmel, *Mussolini. L'uomo e l'opera* (Florence, 1954), III, 299.
85. Emil Ludwig, *Colloqui con Mussolini* (Milan, 1965), 89.
86. *Antieuropa*, October–December, 1933.
87. *Ibid.*
88. *Ibid.*
89. For example, in 1934 the GUF attempted to organize a meeting where European youth could organize "in order to comprehend the horizons which Mussolini opens up to Europe."

Gravelli was predictably furious at this attempt to usurp his own position. Cf. *Ottobre*, May 2, 1934.

Chapter Four: *The Fascist International*

1. On Mussolini's foreign prestige, cf. Santarelli, *op. cit.*, 101–132.
2. Guido De Luca, "La nuova generazione belga," in *Critica Fascista*, August 15, 1933.
3. Zangrandi, "I giovani e il fascismo," *op. cit.*, 212.
4. Zangrandi, *Il lungo viaggio, op. cit.*, 226.
5. *Ibid.*
6. *Ibid.*
7. Duilio Susmel, *Vita Sbagliata di Galeazzo Ciano* (Milan, 1962), 44.
8. Asvero Gravelli, *Panfascismo* (Rome, 1935), 353.
9. Cf. *Ottobre*, July 16–31, 1933.
10. *Ibid.*
11. *Ibid.*
12. *Ibid.*
13. Eugenio Coselschi, *Universalità del Fascismo* (Florence, 1933), 7.
14. Del Boca and Giovana, *op. cit.*, 63–64.
15. De Felice, *Storia degli ebrei, op. cit.*, 147–158.
16. *Ottobre*, May 1, 1934.
17. *Ibid.*
18. *Ibid.*, May 4, 1934.
19. Horia Sima, *La destinée du nationalisme* (Paris, 1949), 73.
20. ACS, *Minculpop*, Busta 115, f. 2.
21. Cited in Del Boca and Giovana, *loc. cit.*
22. Gravelli, *Panfascismo, op. cit.*, 296–316.
23. *Ibid.*
24. *Ibid.*
25. Cf. *Ottobre*, March 15, 1935.
26. *Ibid.*, November 30, 1932.
27. This is supported by Klaus-Peter Hoepke, *Die deutsche Rechte und der italienische Faschismus* (Düsseldorf, 1968), 259–265. Cf. also Alan Cassels, "Mussolini and German Nationalism," in the *Journal of Modern History*, June, 1963.
28. Cf. De Felice, "Una pagina ignota," *op. cit.*

29. Comitati d'azione per la universalità di Roma, *Reunion de Montreux 16–17 Decembre, 1934–XIII* (Rome, 1935), 3.
30. *Ibid.*, 32.
31. *Ibid.*
32. *Ottobre*, September 1, 1933.
33. Comitati d'azione, *loc. cit.*
34. *Ibid.*, 40.
35. *Ibid.*, 36.
36. *Ibid.*, 77–79.
37. *Ibid.*, 81.
38. *Ibid.*, 82.
39. *Ibid.*, 83.
40. *Ibid.*, 84.
41. *Ibid.*, 83.
42. *Ibid.*
43. *Ibid.*, 84.
44. *Ibid.*
45. *Ibid.*, 85.
46. *Ibid.*
47. *Ibid.*, 86.
48. *Ibid.*
49. *Ibid.*, 87.
50. *Ibid.*
51. *Ibid.*
52. Cf. Del Boca and Giovana, *op. cit.*, 71.
53. *Ottobre*, February 2, 1935.
54. Cf. Del Boca and Giovana, *loc. cit.*
55. *Ottobre*, April 2, 1935.
56. ACS, *Minculpop*, Busta 181, f. 7.
57. *Ibid.*
58. *Ibid.*
59. *Ottobre*, February 2, 1935.
60. Santarelli, *op. cit.*, 147.
61. *Ibid.*
62. The most important such group was at the University of Perugia, and included some members of the *Circolo filologico milanese*. Ferri himself contributed to a volume of essays published there on Corporate doctrine.
63. Chabod, *loc. cit.*

64. *Universalità Fascista,* June, 1935.
65. *Ibid.*
66. ACS, *Segr. part. del Duce, cart. ris. (1922–1943),* Busta 59, fasc. W/R, *Fantini.*
67. Cf. *Universalità Fascista,* January, 1936.
68. Zangrandi, *op. cit.,* 145–150.
69. Salvatorelli and Mira, *op. cit.,* 810.
70. Cf. Jedlicka, *loc. cit.*
71. Cf. Zangrandi, "I giovani e il fascismo," *loc. cit.*

Chapter Five: *Beyond the International*

1. F. W. Deakin, *The Brutal Friendship* (New York, 1962), 6–8.
2. Cf., for example, Zangrandi, *op. cit.,* 31.
3. Cf. Chabod, *op. cit.,* 97.
4. Zangrandi, "I giovani e il fascismo," *op. cit.,* 212.
5. De Felice, *Storia degli ebrei, op. cit.,* 18–20.
6. Quoted *ibid.,* 25.
7. Quoted *ibid.,* 83.
8. Chaim Weizmann, *La mia vita per Israele* (Milan, 1950), 405–407.
9. *Israel,* November 3, 1927, quoted in De Felice, *Storia degli ebrei, op. cit.,* 109.
10. De Felice, *Storia degli ebrei, op. cit.,* 90–100.
11. *Atti Parlamentari, Camera dei Deputati.* Seduta del 13 maggio, 1929.
12. Cf. De Felice, *Storia degli ebrei, op. cit.,* 115.
13. *Ibid.*
14. Hubert Lagardelle, *Mission à Rome. Mussolini* (Paris, 1955), 84.
15. Quoted in De Felice, *Storia degli ebrei, op. cit.,* 148.
16. *Ibid.*
17. *Ibid.,* 152–153.
18. *Ibid.,* 157.
19. Cf. *Protocole de la troisième Conférence Juive Mondiale. Genève 20–23 août 1934* (Paris, 1934), 108–109.
20. De Felice, *Storia degli ebrei, op. cit.,* 158.
21. Cf. Cassels, *op. cit.*
22. Roberto Guariglia, *Ricordi* (Naples, 1949), 328.
23. De Felice, *Storia degli ebrei, op. cit.,* 211–228. Also Felix Gil-

bert, "Ciano and his Ambassadors," in Gordon A. Craig and Felix Gilbert, eds., *The Diplomats 1919–1939* (New York, 1965), II, 512–536.

24. Gilbert, *op. cit.*, 512–513.
25. De Felice, *Storia degli ebrei, op. cit.*, 281–290.
26. ACS, *Emilio De Bono (diari)*, q. 43, 4 settembre, 1938.
27. Leto, *op. cit.*, 138 ff.
28. De Felice, *Storia degli ebrei, op. cit.*, 286–287.
29. Cf. Asvero Gravelli, *Mussolini Aneddotico* (Rome, 1951).
30. *Il Messaggero di Rodi*, August 22, 1938.
31. ACS, *Minculpop*, Busta 6, fasc. 62, *Istituto Europa Giovane*.
32. *Ibid.*
33. *Ibid.*
34. De Felice, *Storia degli ebrei, op. cit.*, 284.
35. Cited in *ibid.*, 329.
36. Luti, *op. cit.*, 222–223.
37. Zangrandi, *Il lungo viaggio, op. cit.*, 398–400.
38. *Ibid.*, 149–159.
39. Luti, *op. cit.*, 249.
40. *Ibid.*, 221–224.
41. Cf. Galeazzo Ciano, *Diario 1939–1943* (Milan, 1963), I, 5.
42. Cf. above, 117–120.
43. I have been able to see only one issue, dated September, 1942, in the Biblioteca Centrale Nazionale, Florence. Also cf. the interview with Coselschi on the use of racism by the CAUR in *L'ambrosiano*, September 7, 1938.
44. Cf., for example, *Universalità Fascista*, November, 1936.
45. Biagio Scuderi, "Politica demografica nazional-socialista," in *Universalità Fascista*, August, 1937.
46. ACS, *Minculpop*, Busta 84, fasc. 1, *Atti vari della Scuola di Mistica Fascista Sandro Italico Mussolini*. Also De Felice, *Storia degli ebrei italiani, op. cit.*, 438.
47. De Felice, *Storia degli ebrei italiani, op. cit.*, 449.
48. *Ibid.*, 294.
49. *Ibid., loc. cit.*
50. Quoted in A. James Gregor, *The Ideology of Fascism* (New York, 1969), 279.
51. Galeazzo Ciano, *Diario 1937–1938* (Rome, 1956), *passim*.
52. De Felice, *Storia degli ebrei, op. cit.*, 298.

53. Yvon De Begnac, *Palazzo Venezia—Storia di un Regime* (Rome, 1950), 643.
54. Cf., for example, the article by Giuseppe Scudero, "Mussolini spirito europeo."
55. Giuseppe Chiarelli, "I valori universali del fascismo," in *Universalità Fascista*, October, 1937.
56. Carlo Curcio, "Aspetti universali della politica sociale fascista," in *Universalità Fascista*, October, 1937.
57. Oddone Fantini, "Alle basi della dottrina fascista," in *Universalità Fascista*, October, 1937.
58. *Ibid.*
59. Cf. Zangrandi, *Il lungo viaggio, op. cit.*, 217–238.
60. *Ibid.*, 13–19.
61. Spinetti, *Vent'anni dopo, op. cit.*, 65.
62. *Ibid.*

Conclusion: *The Incomplete Revolution*

1. William Bolitho, *Italy under Mussolini* (New York, 1926), 51.
2. De Felice, ed., *Fascismo e Partiti Politici, op. cit.*, 10–12.
3. Salvatorelli and Mira, *op. cit.*, 413.
4. Finer, *op. cit.*, i.
5. *Ibid.*
6. De Felice, *Mussolini il fascista. I, La conquista del potere 1921–1925* (Turin, 1966), 77–78.
7. Quoted in Lyttelton, *op. cit.*, 77.
8. Mosse, "Fascism and the Intellectuals," *op. cit.*, 208.
9. Introduction to Nolte, *op. cit.*
10. Mosse, "Fascism and the Intellectuals," *op. cit.*, 216–217.
11. Camillo Pellizzi, *Una Rivoluzione Mancata* (Milan, 1949), 18.
12. *Ibid.*, 57.

BIBLIOGRAPHY

⋏⋏⋏ It would be superfluous to list all the works consulted for this book; I have therefore named only those works that have been of substantial help. The Bibliography is not intended to be comprehensive, but rather a useful guide to the available literature. No articles in English are listed, since the handful which were found to be of use are listed in the Notes.

I. Documentary Sources

The indispensable source for material on the doctrine of *fascismo universale* is the journals of the movement. They are: *Antieuropa, Critica Fascista, Ottobre, Il Saggiatore, La Sapienza, L'Universale, Universalità Fascista,* and *Universalità Romana.*

In addition, two newspapers are fundamental to an understanding of the fascist period in Italy: *Il Popolo d'Italia,* the "official" paper of the regime, and *Il Corriere della Sera* of Milan, which maintained a certain autonomy even during the most oppressive periods of censorship.

The best collection of Mussolini's speeches and letters has recently been completed, and provides a solid basis for dealing with the dictator's positions from day to day: Edoardo and Duilio Susmel, eds., *Opera Omnia di Benito Mussolini* (Florence, 1954–63).

The documents of the Fascist Regime are available to scholars in the Archivio Centrale dello Stato (E.U.R.) in Rome. The two most useful collections which I have consulted are: *Segretaria particolare del Duce, carteggio riservato (1922–1943)* and *Ministero della cultura popolare.*

II. Books Published During the *Ventennio*

Ardemagni, Mirko: *La Francia sarà fascista?* (Milan, 1937).
Bacaloglu, Elena: *Movimento nazionale fascista italo-rumeno* (Milan, 1923).
Barnes, James Strachey: *The Universal Aspects of Fascism* (London, 1928).
Battaglia, Tommaso: *Essenza universale del Fascismo* (Salerno, 1935).
Bizzarro, Ruggiero: *Il Fascismo e la sua espansione nel mondo* (Capri, 1933).
Bottai, Giuseppe: *Sviluppi dell'idea corporativa nella legislazione internazionale* (Livorno, 1928).
Coceani, Bruno: *Il Fascismo nel mondo* (Rocca S. Casciano, 1933).
Coppola, Francesco: *La Rivoluzione Fascista e la politica mondiale* (Rome, 1923).
Coselschi, Eugenio: *L'Oriente e l'Occidente nella romanità* (Rome, n.d.).
————: *Universalità del fascismo* (Florence, 1933).
Curcio, Carlo: *Verso la nuova Europa* (Naples, 1936).
De Miege, M. R.: *La dottrina del Fascismo in Inghilterra* (Rome, 1933).
Di Marzio, Cornelio: *Il Fascismo all'estero* (Milan, 1923).
Ercole, Francesco: *La Rivoluzione fascista* (Palermo, n.d.).
Fanelli, G. A.: *Discorso agli italiani. Manifesto agli europei* (Rome, 1930).
Fantini, Oddone: *L'universalità del Fascismo* (Naples, 1933).
Gianni, Niccolò: *La marcia ideale sul mondo della civilta fascista* (Milan, 1933).
Grandi, Dino: *L'Italia fascista nella politica internazionale* (Rome, 1930).
Gravelli, Asvero: *Difesa dell'Europa e funzione antieuropa del Fascismo* (Rome, 1932).
————: *Europa con noi!* (Rome, 1933).
————: *La marche de Rome et l'Europe* (Rome, 1932).
————: *Panfascismo* (Rome, 1935).
————: *Verso l'internazionale fascista* (Rome, 1932).
Knickerbocker, Hubert Rempo: *Il Fascismo inglese e la ripresa economica dell'Inghilterra* (Milan, 1935).

Lojacono, Luigi: *Il Fascismo nel mondo* (Rome, 1933).

Luchini, Alberto: *I falangisti spagnuoli* (Florence, n.d.).

Maraviglia, M.: *Il nuovo valore spirituale ed internazionale dell' Italia* (Rome, 1924).

Maresca della Salandra di Serracapriola, Giovanni: *L'universalità del Fascismo. Discorso* (Rome, 1933).

Marpicati, Arturo: *Fondamenti ideali e storici del Fascismo* (Bologna, 1931).

Murri, Romolo: *L'idea universale di Roma. Dalle origini al fascismo* (Milan, 1937).

Mussolini, Arnaldo: *Verso il nuovo primato* (Milan, 1929).

Nanni, Torquato: *Bolscevismo e Fascismo al lume della critica marxista. Benito Mussolini* (Bologna, 1924).

Nardelli, Matteo: *Fascismo, idea universale* (Trento, 1936).

Paresce, Gabriele: *Espansione del corporativismo all'estero* (Rome, 1934).

Pedrazzi, Orazio: *Roma alla testa del mondo* (Santiago del Cile, 1933).

Rapicavoli, Carmelo: *La missione universale di Roma* (Bologna, 1936).

Scorza, Carlo: *Fascismo idea imperiale* (Rome, 1933).

Spinetti, Gastone Silvano: *L'Europa verso la Rivoluzione* (Rome, 1936).

———: *Fascismo universale* (Rome, 1933).

———: *Fascismo e Libertà* (Padua, 1941).

Valois, Georges: *Il Fascismo francese: cio che siamo, da dove veniamo? Dove andiamo?* (Rome, 1926).

Varo, Arminio: *Verso gli Stati Uniti fascisti d'Europa* (Milan, 1932).

Vicenti, Luigi: *Il Fascismo nei riflessi della stampa estera* (Milan, 1924).

Villa, Oreste: *L'America latina. Problema fascista* (Rome, 1933).

III. Articles Published During the *Ventennio*

The following is a representative selection, intended to supplement those already mentioned in the text.

Ardemagni, Mirco: "Fascismo, rivoluzione continentale," in *Gerarchia*, Anno XIV, 1934, 124 ff.

Caparelli, Filippo: "Testimonianze straniere sul Fascismo," in *Gerarchia*, Anno XIII, 1933, 112 ff.

Curcio, Carlo: "Lamarcia sul mondo," in *Lo Stato*, Anno IV, 1933, 90 ff.

———: "Verso la nuova Europa," in *Lo Stato*, Anno II, 1931, 19 ff.

De Marsanich, Augusto: "Universalità dell'idea corporativa," in *Politica Sociale*, Anno VI, 1934, 469 ff.

Di Pretorio, Francesco: "Fascismo realtà universale," in *La Stirpe*, Anno XI, 1933, 384 ff.

Fantini, Oddone: "Caratteri universali del Fascismo," extract from *La Giustizia del Lavoro*, 1932.

———: "Romanità e Fascismo" Conference, Perugia, 1932.

Ferretti, Lando: "Universalità del Fascismo," in *Gerarchia*, Anno XI, 1931, 104 ff.

Ferri, Carlo Emilio: "Il Fascismo negli Stati del Nord-Europa," in *Gerarchia*, Anno XII, 1932, 868 ff.

Govi, Mario: "Per l'espansione del Fascismo," in *Critica Fascista*, Anno VIII, 1930, 263 ff.

Guglielmotti, Umberto: "Conquiste del Fascismo e riconoscimenti stranieri," in *Assicurazioni Sociali*, 1935, 453 ff.

Manoilesco, Mihail: "L'avvenire del Fascismo nel mondo," in *Politica sociale*, Anno VI, 1934, 461 ff.

Messina, Arnaldo: "Universalità del Fascismo," in *Educazione Fascista*, Anno IX, 1931, 883 ff.

Mosley, Oswald: "Il Fascismo come fattore di pace universale," in *Gerarchia*, Anno XII, 1932, 861 ff.

Pietri, Paolo: "Tentativi di imitazione fascista in Jugoslavia," in *Gerarchia*, Anno XII, 1932, 830 ff.

Rohan, K. A.: "Fascismo in Austria," in *Gerarchia*, Anno XII, 1932, 821 ff.

Rossi, Ettore: "Il Fascismo nel vicino Oriente," in *Gerarchia*, Anno XII, 1932, 843 ff.

Selvi, Giovanni: "Fermentazione fascista nel mondo," in *Gerarchia*, Anno XIII, 1933, 933 ff.

Valentini, Giuseppe: "Il Corporativismo in Portogallo," in *Gerarchia*, Anno XIV, 1934, 290 ff.

IV. Secondary Works

Aquarone, Alberto: *L'organizzazione dello Stato totalitario* (Turin, 1965).

Bardeche, Maurice: *Qu'est-ce que le fascisme?* (Paris, 1961).

Bottai, Giuseppe: *Vent'anni e un giorno* (Rome, 1949).

Chabod, Federico: *L'Italia Contemporanea (1918–1948)* (Turin, 1968).

Ciano, Galeazzo: *Diario (1939–1943)* (Milan, 1963).

D'Aroma, Nino: *Mussolini Segreto* (Rocca S. Casciano, 1958).

Deakin, F. W.: *The Brutal Friendship* (New York, 1962).

De Felice, Renzo: *Mussolini il fascista. I, La conquista del potere, 1921–1925* (Turin, 1966).

———: *Mussolini il fascista. II, L'organizzazione dello Stato fascista* (Turin, 1968).

———: *Storia degli ebrei italiani sotto il fascismo* (Turin, 1961).

Del Boca, Angelo, and Giovana, Mario: *I "figli del sole"* (Milan, 1965).

Finer, Herman: *Mussolini's Italy* (New York, 1965).

Georges-Roux: *Vita di Mussolini* (Rome, 1961).

Harris, H. S.: *The Social Philosophy of Giovanni Gentile* (Urbana, Ill., and London, 1966).

Hoepke, Klaus-Peter: *Die deutsche Rechte und der italienische Faschismus* (Düsseldorf, 1968).

Jacini, Stefano: *Il regime fascista* (n.p., 1947).

Leto, Guido: *OVRA. Fascismo-antifascismo* (Bologna, 1962).

Luti, Giorgio: *Cronache letterarie tra le due guerre 1920/1940* (Bari, 1966).

Martinelli, S.: *L'OVRA* (Milan, 1967).

Megaro, Gaudens: *Mussolini in the Making* (New York, 1967).

Mosse, George L., and Laqueur, Walter, eds.: *International Fascism 1920–1945* (New York, 1966).

Nolte, Ernst: *Three Faces of Fascism* (New York, 1966).

Pellizzi, Camillo: *Una Rivoluzione Mancata* (Milan, 1949).

Rocca, Massimo: *Il Primo Fascismo* (Rome, 1964).

Rossi, Ernesto: *Padroni del vapore e fascismo* (Bari, 1966).

Salvatorelli, Luigi, and Mira, Giovanni, *Storia d'Italia nel periodo fascista* (Turin, 1961).

Salvemini, Gaetano: *Under the Axe of Fascism* (New York, 1967).

Santarelli, Enzo: *Storia del movimento e del regime fascista* (Rome, 1967).

Villari, Luigi: *Italian Foreign Policy under Mussolini* (New York, 1956).

Woolf, Stuart, ed., *European Fascism* (London, 1968).

————: *The Nature of Fascism* (London, 1968).

INDEX

Index [*197*

Palestine and Zionism, 119, 137–8, 140

Keller, 113
Korherr, Richard, 102

labor, 65–6, 91
Labor Charter, 75
Labriola, Arturo, 4
La Rosa, Mario, 52
Lateran Pact, *see* Concordat
Lausanne, 86–90
League of Nations, 98
Légion Nationale Belge (National Legion of Belgium), 114, 119, 129
Lenin, 58
Ligue Corporative du Travail, 114, 119
Lithuania, 115
Loutkie, Wouter, 119, 128
Lozzi, Carlo, 124–7, 133
Luzzatti, Luigi, 136

Machiavelli, Niccolò, 56
Mack Smith, Denis, xiii, xx
Manacorda, Guido, 40
Mannhardt, J. W., 87
Manoilesco, Mihail, 82, 145
March on Rome, 18, 20, 26, 28, 70, 156–7, 159, 162
Marinetti, Emilio F. T., 4–7, 9, 60
Marpicati, Arturo, 38
Matteotti, Giacomo, 6, 9–10, 64
Mazzini, Giuseppe, 3, 4, 9, 17, 59, 84, 85, 103, 161
Mein Kampf (Hitler), 101
Mercouris, Georges, 115, 119, 122–4
Meyer, Arnold, 115, 125, 128
Milan, 78, 85–6, 92
Minculpop, 15, 22, 39, 47, 52, 93, 145

Missiroli, Mario, 150
Montreux Congress, xviii–xix, 114–29, 133, 139, 144, 161, 163–5
morality, 18–19, 49–51, 94–5
Mosley, Oswald, 113
Mosse, George L., xi–xii, 162–3, 165
Motza, Ion, 115, 118–20, 126
Mussert, 100, 123
Mussolini, Arnaldo, 57, 145; Christianity, 58, 90; universal fascism, 19–24, 33, 108; youth and, 18–25, 32, 36–9, 44, 51, 55, 70, 98
Mussolini, Benito, 28, 31, 46, 50, 57, 81, 88, 89, 95, 106, 129–30; anti-Nazism, 98, 101–2, 114; Corporativism, 66, 72–3; economics, 65–6, 112; effectiveness of fascist rule, 14; Fascist International, 99; foreign policy, 98–100, 107, 131–4, 137 ff.; Gentile and, 46; Hitler and, 98–9, 101, 131, 133–4, 139, 165; ideology, 24, 157 ff.; Jewish question, 101, 135–55 *passim*, 166–7; obedience and loyalty to, 47, 144, 148; popularity, 67, 73, 83–4, 168; post-*Risorgimento* politics, xvi–xvii; power structure, 64 ff., 73; propaganda, 93, 102; universal fascism and, xviii, xix, 19, 23, 33, 60–3, 72–3, 76 ff., 97, 102, 104–5, 111 ff., 131, 163–4; and youth, 3–4, 12 ff., 29, 60, 69–71, 107, 130–1
Mussolini, Sandro Italico, 18, 20
Mussolini, Vittorio, 22, 37–9, 134, 168
Mussolini's Italy (Finer), 157–8
mysticism, fascist, 18 ff., 47–8, 122, 148

Nasjonal Samling, 115
Nasti, Agostino, 32–3
Nationaal Socialistische Beweging, 123
National Corpset, 114, 125

*Typography, binding and
jacket design by
Albert Burkhardt*